(PER)VERSIONS OF LOVE AND HATE

WO ES WAR

A series from Verso edited by Slavoj Žižek

Wo es war, soll ich werden – Where it was, I shall come into being – is Freud's version of the Enlightenment goal of knowledge that is in itself an act of liberation. Is it still possible to pursue this goal today, in the conditions of late capitalism? If 'it' today is the twin rule of pragmatic-relativist New Sophists and New Age obscurantists, what 'shall come into being' in its place? The premiss of the series is that the explosive combination of Lacanian psychoanalysis and Marxist tradition detonates a dynamic freedom that enables us to question the very presuppositions of the circuit of Capital.

(PER)VERSIONS OF LOVE AND HATE

RENATA SALECL

VERSO

London • New York

In memory of my dear friend Frida Saal (Talila)

First published by Verso 1998
© Renata Salecl 1998
Paperback edition first published by Verso 2000
© Renata Salecl 2000
All rights reserved

Verso
UK: 6 Meard Street, London W1V 3HR
US: 180 Varick Street, New York, NY 10014–4606

Verso is the imprint of New Left Books

ISBN 1–85984–236–4

British Library Cataloguing in Publication Data
A catalogue record for this book is available from the British Library

Library of Congress Cataloging-in-Publication Data
A catalog record for this book is available from the Library of Congress

Typeset by SetSystems Ltd, Saffron Walden, Essex
Printed by Biddles Ltd, Guildford and King's Lynn

CONTENTS

ACKNOWLEDGEMENTS

Preliminary versions of some of the material contained in this book were previously published as essays in various journals and books. Chapter 1 appeared in *Gaze and Voice as Love Objects*, edited by Renata Salecl and Slavoj Žižek (Durham, NC: Duke University Press 1996). Parts of Chapters 2 and 4 were published in *Journal for the Psychoanalysis of Culture and Society* 1 and 2 (Spring and Fall 1996). An early version of Chapter 3 appeared in *Differences* 1 (Spring 1997), and in *Cogito and the Unconscious*, edited by Slavoj Žižek (Durham, NC: Duke University Press 1998). Chapter 5 was published in *Law and the Postmodern Mind*, edited by Peter Goodrich and David Gray Carlson (Ann Arbor: University of Michigan Press 1998). Chapter 6 was an essay in *Radical Evil*, edited by Joan Copjec (London: Verso 1996).

INTRODUCTION: FROM *ETERNITY* TO *CONTRADICTION*

In high fashion, the dominant trend of recent years has been the so-called new simplicity: clothes are unpretentious in style, colors are dark and the designer's name is not displayed on the outside of a garment.[1] The goal of this style is to accentuate the individual's inner qualities; the dress just helps the individual to express what he or she is. Thus it does not try to change the individual into someone else or create an image in which the individual would like to see him- or herself; it merely enhances his or her already existing individuality. Today, the individual is not supposed to buy high fashion in order to follow some imposed ideal of beauty, but rather to aid perception of him- or herself as an ideal.

The emergence of this ideology of a new individuality can best be illustrated by analyzing the change in the naming of Calvin Klein's perfumes. A list of these names can help us trace a genealogy of the perception of subjectivity in contemporary society. Some years ago, Klein produced perfumes named *Eternity*, *Escape* and *Obsession*. When we hear the word *Eternity* we immediately think about something timeless: perfume with such a name alludes to what is beyond the subject's bodily constraints. By using the perfume *Escape*, the subject also evades the misery of his or her everyday life. An escape from this misery might come with the help of magic love, which the subject can incite by using the perfume *Obsession*. All three perfumes are advertised with images of beautiful, half-naked young men and women. These images have explicit sexual connotations and also allude to something beyond the agony of our everyday existence. The advertisements accept sexual difference (so we have male and female versions of the same perfume) and use of the perfume is supposed to make the sexes more attractive to each other.

In the nineties, discussions in the domain of post-structuralism and gender theory contributed to a radical change in the perception of sexual difference. In theoretical circles, it became fashionable to emphasize that sexual difference is socially constructed and performatively enacted. Paradoxically, fashion started following this trend, to the point of stressing the utter bisexuality of the subject. Contemporary design accordingly became asexual. Calvin Klein followed this new trend with a perfume, *One*, which can be used by men and by women. The advertisements for this perfume show young androgenic people whose sexual identity is difficult to discern. This asexual trend continues with the next Klein perfume – *Be* – which was advertised with the slogan: "To be. Not to be. Just be." The advertising posters still show images of androgynous youth, but now they look like worn-out crack addicts.

In the past, the names of perfumes alluded to the secret of the subject's charm: what is in the woman more than herself is her *Trésor* (Lancôme), which can also be understood as *Tendre poison* (Dior). These names indicated the nature of the precious object in the subject: this object resembles a perfume's whiff – it is nothing one can physically discern, but it is alluring and poisonous at the same time. If designers of these old perfumes tried to figure out how to depict the nature of the libidinal object in the subject, contemporary perfume fashion follows the trend of so-called *identity politics*. Here the problem is no longer how to depict the nature of the sublime object in the subject, which is beyond the subject's grasp; today, the subject is the entity that has to be promoted as a whole. This subject, of course, is not monolithic, but someone who is always changing his or her identity. The nature of this change is best exemplified by the latest Calvin Klein perfume, *Contradiction*, which is advertised with the slogan: "She is always and never the same."

Subjects today no longer believe in the normative ideals offered by society and instead take themselves to be creators of their own identities. (This trend is illustrated in the advertising for the new Hugo Boss perfume *Hugo Woman*, which urges: "Don't imitate. Innovate.") However, the fact that today the subject is supposed to have every possibility to make out of him- or herself a "work of art" does not make him or her feel free from social constraints. Although the subject may no longer believe in the old authorities that regulate his or her life, the subject nonetheless searches for new points of identification and invents new rules to regulate the horrible nature of this newly acquired freedom to be just "oneself".

The change in the naming of the perfumes thus illuminates the nature of the change in the perception of contemporary subjectivity. How does the subject today deal with the traumatic nature of the lack in him- or herself, and the Other, insofar as the subject actually believes in the possibility of freely fashioning his or her identity without reference to the Other? And what kind of change do we encounter today in intersubjective relations, when subjects no longer identify with the authorities in the way they used to? These questions are addressed by analyzing various cases of love and hate in contemporary society, taking examples from novels, movies and political debates.

The book, whose central topic can be summarized in Lacan's famous saying, "I love you, but, because inexplicably I love in you something more than you – the *objet petit a* – I mutilate you",[2] starts with the issue of desire and love. Why does the subject who is desperately in love endlessly block union with his or her love-object? Chapter 1 analyzes this deadlock of love with the help of Wharton's *The Age of Innocence* and Ishiguro's *The Remains of the Day*. The psychoanalytic notion of desire is very much linked to non-satisfaction, which means that we desire things because they are unavailable; and to keep desire alive, the subject needs to prevent its fulfillment. In this search for the impossible object, desire is, of course, very much linked to the issue of love. But love also concerns another psychoanalytic notion – the notion of libido or drive, which, with its destructive nature, much more radically determines the subject's passionate attachments. Chapter 2 explains this move from desire to drive, referring to a series of classic Hollywood melodramas (*Rhapsody*, *Seventh Veil*, *The Red Shoes* and *Humoresque*). And Chapter 3 deals with the seductive nature of the female drive, as depicted in the story of the Sirens' deadly song.

The object that is in one more than oneself is therefore to be understood as the object of desire as well as the object of drive. In both cases, the object can simultaneously be perceived as something one admires and is seduced by, as well as something one hates and is disgusted by. Paradoxically, the subject often destroys what he or she most loves. This is the case not only in the subject's private life; passionate attachments to one's country can also lead to its destruction. Chapter 4 shows how Ceauşescu's attitude toward Romania can be summarized with the saying: "I love my country, that is why I mutilate it."

In today's tolerant multicultural universe, it is usually assumed that the last defense against this self-destructive fury of love–hate is respect for others: from differing life styles within our society, through respect for other races and nations, to respect for animals. Chapter 5 analyzes the famous case of the Russian artist Oleg Kulik, who plays a dog in art

galleries and occasionally bites members of his audience. Kulik's performances help us find an explanation of why even dogs that bite are often
easier to love than other human beings.

When we praise the need for tolerance and respect in our society, the
question is also: what kind of other do the multiculturalists really tolerate
and respect? Isn't it a very particular kind of other – the other as victim –
that attracts the multiculturalists' attention? When the other ceases to play
the role of a passive victim and starts to act in ways that surprise Western
observers, he or she quickly becomes designated as an enemy – as totalitarian, fundamentalist, etc. Chapters 6 and 7 analyze how love for the other
turns into hate by taking examples from contemporary political debates on
racism and multiculturalism. Chapter 6 engages the issue of hate speech. It
analyzes the dilemma of how to deal with different cultures' radically
different ways of perceiving violence and with differences in the understanding of the universals (human rights, equality, freedom, etc.) on behalf
of which societies try to prevent violence. The exemplary case of such
violence is female circumcision. Chapter 7 questions whether this kind of
female genital mutilation is simply a question of choice and why we
encounter a return to these practices of initiation among some immigrants
in the West. This problem is analyzed in the context of other forms of
marking the body with a cut in contemporary society, like some types of
body art, tattooing or body piercing.

The book starts with an analysis of love that pertains more to modern
society, but the conclusion deals with the contours of love and hate in post-
modern society. Today a radical change has happened in the subject's
identification with the symbolic order, the so-called big Other. In post-
modern society, people no longer believe in the fiction of the big Other as
they did in modern or pre-modern society. But disbelief in the big Other
does not simply bring liberation for the subject; it also triggers regression
into various forms of violence, including self-mutilation. By these practices,
some people are acting in accordance with the idea that today everything is
changeable and that life resembles a computer screen on which the subject
can randomly choose his or her identity. But others are using similar forms
of self-mutilation as a reaction against the ideology of changeable identities.

The return to the cut in the body is to be understood as a specific way in
which the contemporary subject deals with his or her lack, as well as with
the lack in the Other. These practices of body mutilation should not be
taken as proofs of some kind of generalized perversion of contemporary

society; they are rather a symptom of the radical change that has affected subjectivity.

I thank Jane Malmo and Mitch Cohen for correcting my translation and making many helpful comments. The book was completed during my stay at the Wissenschaftskolleg in Berlin; I am most grateful for the perfect working conditions provided there.

NOTES

1. The most renowned propagators of the new simplicity in fashion are Georgio Armani, Donna Karan, Calvin Klein and Jill Sander.
2. Jacques Lacan, *The Four Fundamental Concepts of Psycho-Analysis*, trans. Alan Sheridan, New York: Norton 1977, p. 263.

1

"I CAN'T LOVE YOU UNLESS I GIVE YOU UP"

"Love for oneself knows only one barrier – love for others, love for objects." (Sigmund Freud, *Group Psychology and the Analysis of the Ego*)

One of the greatest illusions about love is that prohibition and social codes prevent its realization. The illusionary character of this proposition is unveiled in every "self-help" manual: the advice people desperately in love usually get is to establish artificial barriers, prohibitions, and to make themselves temporarily inaccessible in order to provoke their love-object to return love. Or, as Freud said: "Some obstacle is necessary to swell the tide of the libido to its heights; and in all periods of history, wherever natural barriers in the way of satisfaction have not sufficed, mankind has erected conventional ones in order to be able to enjoy love."[1] What is the nature of these barriers? What is the role of institutions, rituals and social codes in relation to the subject's innermost passions, their love? And why does the subject persist in loving a person who has no intention of returning love?

I will try to answer these questions by taking the example, first, of two novels, Kazuo Ishiguro's *The Remains of the Day* and Edith Wharton's *The Age of Innocence*, and, second, of a short story by Edith Wharton, "The Muse's Tragedy". While the latter deals with a woman using the love of a man to organize the symbolic space that would provide her with an identity and confirm her as an object of love, the two novels are about the opposite problem of love supposedly thwarted by society's symbolic power structure. Let me first focus on the novels, which offer an aesthetic presentation of what Louis Althusser called Ideological State Apparatuses (ISAs): "a certain number of realities which present themselves to the immediate observer in the form of distinct and specialist institutions" and are primarily part of the private domain, like families, schools, churches, parties or cultural ventures.² In the two novels, it is precisely one of the most important ISAs, the family and "society", in the sense of codified social norms and the hierarchy of social relations, that dominates the private life of the protagonists: their love affairs are supposedly constrained by the influence of the oppressive ISAs that organize their lives.

The Age of Innocence is set in the extremely hierarchical high society of nineteenth-century New York, where every social act or movement is codified, and where it can be a constant struggle for an individual not to misinterpret the unwritten rules and become an outcast. The extent of codification in this society is visible in the way people organize their public and private lives: from the type of china they use at dinner parties, to the way they dress, the location of their houses, the respect they pay to people higher up the social ladder, etc. *The Remains of the Day* is set in the equally hierarchical aristocratic society of England just before and after the Second World War, with the central role played by the highest of servants – the butler. This is also a society of unwritten codes, in which every part of life is fully organized. And the butler is the one upon whom the perfection and maintenance of this order depends. As the butler Stevens in *The Remains of the Day* points out, by doing his service in the most dignified and perfectionist manner, he contributes significantly to the major historical events his master is involved in. The butler Stevens is the prototype of an "ideological servant": he never questions his role in the machinery, he never opposes his boss even when he makes obvious mistakes, i.e. he does not think but obeys.

Both novels imply there is something suppressed or hidden behind this ideological machinery – the passions of the individuals engaged in these rituals, their secret "true" loves. The film versions of the two novels especially stress this hidden terrain "beneath" the institution, the "real" emotions behind the fake, public ones. The main trauma of *The Age of Innocence* is thus the impossibility of love between Newland Archer, the young aristocrat, and Countess Ellen Olenska, the eccentric woman whose behavior is under the close scrutiny of New York society. Newland, who is engaged to be married to one of the "proper" women of this society, tacitly, because of its rules, gives up his hopes of fulfilling his desire for Ellen and becomes a devoted husband. In *The Remains of the Day* we have the unspoken passion between butler Stevens and housekeeper Miss Kenton, both of whom are also too obedient to the social codes to let their feelings out and to find personal happiness. In short, both novels reveal the oppressiveness of the institutions in which their protagonists live, and which prevent them from finding love. The question is, however, whether it is really the institution that prevents love. Is it not actually the institution that, in a paradoxical way, produces love?

THE REMAINS OF THE DAY, OR, LOVE AS PROHIBITION

The Remains of the Day is the story of a butler, Stevens, who has spent his whole life serving in the house of Lord Darlington. In his old age, Stevens takes a trip to visit the housekeeper, Miss Kenton, who had worked in the house twenty years before, with a view to persuading her to return to service in the house. During this trip, Stevens writes a diary in which he recalls his relationship with Miss Kenton and life in the house in the turmoil of the years before the Second World War. These memories of butler Stevens are primarily a tribute to the principles of dignity and morality that define a perfect servant wholly devoted to his master. The subtle character of the novel lies in the fact that emotions are never expressed: although butler Stevens and Miss Kenton care about each other in more than a professional way, they never admit this to each other. Even at the end, when they finally meet again after many years and when there is no actual barrier to their relationship, nothing happens between them. Ritual stays intact and emotions never fully come out – why not?

One interpretation of Stevens's behavior, of his complete repression of emotion, is that he is, in some way, non-human. This is exemplified by his attitude toward his father's death: even as his father is dying, it is more important for Stevens to perform his duties in an impeccable way than to reveal his emotions. Such a humanist interpretation, of course, misses the point of the novel. To understand its logic, one should proceed in the opposite direction: rather than trying to discern the repressed passions that do not come out because of the rigidity of the social system and because of the butler's all too impeccable service, it would be better to begin by taking the ritual and institution seriously and then determine the place love has in them.

How should we understand the title of the novel? A number of explanations are hinted at in the text. First, "the remains of the day" might simply be the memories butler Stevens records in his diary every evening of his journey. The second answer could be that both protagonists are already old, so the "remains" are the few years of life they still have left to them. However, if we draw an analogy between "the remains of the day" and the Freudian "day's residues", a more interesting explanation can be given. In Freud's theory of dreams, the "day's residues" are the events, the residues, of the previous day that acquire a new meaning in dreams because of the unconscious structure into which they get embedded. By reading Stevens's memories in the light of this Freudian concept, it could be said that the remains of the day concern primarily the memory of his relationship with Miss Kenton. The memories that Stevens cherishes the most are of meeting Miss Kenton every evening in their private quarters for cocoa and to discuss the events of the day. These meetings were "the remains of the day" which in Stevens's memory function as residues that he cannot incorporate into the perfect construction of his obsessional style of life. Stevens's relationship with Miss Kenton is therefore the residue around which his unconscious braids, the residue that forces him to confront his desire.

Lacan characterizes the obsessional as one who installs himself in the place of the Other, from where he then acts in a way that prevents any risk of encountering his desire. That is why he invents a number of rituals, self-imposed rules, and organizes his life in a compulsive way. The obsessional also constantly delays decisions in order to escape the risk and uncertainty associated with the desire of the Other, the symbolic order, as well as the concrete other, the opposite sex.

Stevens never admits to himself that he is taking the trip because he wishes to meet Miss Kenton. He finds an excuse for the trip in the lack of servants in the house and in the possibility that he might solve his staff problem by convincing Miss Kenton to return to the house:

> You may be amazed that such an obvious shortcoming to a staff plan should have continued to escape my notice, but then you will agree that such is often the way with matters one has given abiding thought to over a period of time; one is not struck by the truth until prompted quite accidentally by some external event. So it was in this instance; that is to say my receiving the letter from Miss Kenton, containing as it did, along with its long, rather unrevealing passages, an unmistakable nostalgia for Darlington Hall, and – I am quite sure of this – distinct hints of her desire to return here, obliged me to see my staff plan afresh. Only then did it strike me that there was indeed a role that a further staff member could crucially play here; that it was, in fact, this very shortage that had been at the heart of all my recent troubles.

And the more I considered it, the more obvious it became that Miss Kenton, with her great affection for this house, with her exemplary professionalism – the sort almost impossible to find nowadays – was just the factor needed to enable me to complete a fully satisfactory staff plan for Darlington Hall.[3]

This passage is the most profound example of obsessional discourse. To understand Stevens's "real" desire, we have to turn each sentence upside down. The obsessional's speech always suggests meaning that desperately tries to cover his desire, or, more precisely, the obsessional speaks and thinks compulsively only to avoid his desire. When Stevens speaks about the need to solve the staff problem or when he detects in Miss Kenton's letter her wish to return to Darlington Hall, he creates excuses that prevent him from recognizing his own desire. Stevens deposits his desire into the Other: he presents it as the desire of Miss Kenton. The obsessional thus substitutes thought for action and believes that the events in reality are determined by what he thinks. But this omnipotence of thought is linked with a fundamental impotence: "His actions are impotent because he is incapable of engaging himself in an action where he will be recognized by other people."[4] Freud observed that the obsessional's thought process itself becomes sexualized, "for the pleasure which is normally attached to the content of thought becomes shifted onto the act of thinking itself, and the satisfaction derived from reaching the conclusion of a line of thought is experienced as a sexual satisfaction".[5] Stevens thus gets sexual satisfaction from his plan to solve the staff problem by taking the trip to visit Miss Kenton, not from thoughts about Miss Kenton herself.

When Stevens informs his master about his plan to visit Miss Kenton, Lord Darlington mockingly comments that he did not expect his butler still to be interested in women at his age. This remark touches the core of Stevens's desire and he immediately has to organize a ritual to contradict its implication. His conclusion is that Darlington expects Stevens to exchange banter as part of his professional service. Stevens, of course, fails in this task, so he tries to learn the art of witticism: "I have devised a simple exercise which I try to perform at least once a day; whenever an odd moment presents itself, I attempt to formulate three witticisms based on my immediate surroundings at that moment."[6] This is a difficult task because it presents him with the danger of encountering his desire. Stevens knows the danger witticism entails, the fact that its effects are uncontrollable, which is a real horror for an obsessional: "By the very nature of a witticism, one is given very little time to assess its various possible repercussions before one is called to give voice to it, and one gravely risks uttering all manner of unsuitable things if one has not first acquired the necessary skill and experience."[7]

This avoidance of desire is linked to the profession of butler. For Stevens, the high principles of serving as a butler take the form of his Ego Ideal. The most important among them is the "dignity" of the "butler's ability not to abandon the professional being he inhabits".[8] While the lesser butler easily abandons his professional being for the private one, the great butler never does this regardless of the situation: "A butler of any quality must be seen to *inhabit* his role, utterly and fully; he cannot be seen casting it aside one moment simply to do it again the next as though it were nothing more than a pantomime costume."[9] The butler thus has to give duty priority. Jacques-Alain Miller defined the noble as the master who sacrifices his desire to the Ego Ideal. The Ego Ideal is the place in the symbolic order with which the subject identifies. It is the place from which the subject observes himself or herself in the way he or she would like to be seen. For Stevens, this site is the principles or code of the butler's service, or, more precisely, dignity. When the subject sacrifices his desire to the Ideal, when he completely subordinates himself to symbolic identity and takes on a symbolic mask, it is in this mask that one can discern his desire. So when Stevens totally devotes himself to his profession, gives up his private life and renounces any sexual contact with women, when he, therefore, unites himself with the Ideal, it is in this Ideal, in this social mask of decency that his desire reveals itself. The Ideal, which has the meaning of adopting the figure of the Other, is also the other of the subject's desire: the traits of the masks of decency, professionalism and asexuality that form the Ideal are thus co-relative to Stevens's desire. For example, his intended, active ignorance of women can be read as the desire for a woman: "What the subject dissimulates and by means of which he dissimulates, is also the very form of its disclosure."[10]

There is nothing behind the mask: it is in the mask, in the veil that seemingly covers the essence of the subject, that we have to search for this essence. In the case of Stevens, there is no "beyond", no suppressed world of passions hidden behind his mask of proper Englishness.[11] It is useless to search in Stevens for some hidden love that could not come out because of the ritual he rigidly engages in – all his love is in the rituals. If he loves Miss Kenton, he loves her from the perspective of submission to the codes of their profession. Miss Kenton is also a very competent servant, but what actually attracts Stevens to her is her periodical hysterical resistance to the rituals, when she suddenly questions the codes but then again subordinates herself to them.

It would be a mistake to depict Stevens as the only culprit in the non-realization of the love affair. It would be naive to conclude that Miss Kenton would have realized her love for Stevens if only he had been different, more human. Miss Kenton is an example of the hysteric restrained by her paradoxical desire. On the one hand she wants Stevens to change, to reveal his love for her, but, on the other hand, she loves him only for what he actually is – a functionary who tries by all available means to avoid his desire. If Stevens were to change, one might predict that Miss Kenton would quickly abandon him and would despise him, in the same way that she despises her husband.

Miss Kenton develops her first hysterical reaction when a young maid informs her that she is going to marry a fellow servant. Miss Kenton's reaction to this news is very emotional since she herself identifies with the young maid's wish to find love. The young servants realize what Miss Kenton would like to happen between her and Stevens. The next hysterical gesture is Miss Kenton's announcement of her intention to marry Mr. Benn. By this act, as she admits at the end of the novel, Miss Kenton intended to provoke a reaction from Stevens. The hysteric always confronts the question: "What will happen to him if he loses me?" As is further exemplified in Chapters 2 and 3, the paradox of the hysteric's desire is that she wants to have a master, the Other, that she herself can control.

Paradoxically, it is Miss Kenton who actually functions as the support of the institution. She is the *desire* of the institution. This is obvious from her relationship with her husband. When her husband abandons the institution she despises him. She herself cannot endure being outside it. At the end she returns to the institution of the family, although giving reasons outside herself – her husband, her daughter. Nonetheless, this is her true desire.

THE AGE OF INNOCENCE, OR, THE ETHICS OF ROMANTIC LOVE

At first sight, *The Age of Innocence* is a novel of unfulfilled romantic love, of the desperate longing of two people deeply in love (Newland and Ellen) who are unable to pursue their happiness because of the rigid society in which they live. Newland is a conformist, a decent member of New York high society, engaged to be married to May, one of the most eligible girls of this same society. When he encounters the eccentric Ellen and falls in love with her, Newland discovers that there might be something "outside" the societal codes which he so dutifully fulfills. This outside is presumably the world of pure passions, a world where love reigns unconditionally.

The external constraints of the society's codes and the fact that both lovers are married produce the conditions for romantic love to develop. Newland himself admits that the image of Ellen in his memory is stronger than the "real" Ellen. Ellen thus has a special value precisely as absent, inaccessible, as the object of Newland's constant longings. That is why he does not even intend to realize his relationship with her in any sexual form. During one of their emotional encounters, he thus says:

> "Don't be afraid: you needn't squeeze yourself back into your corner like that. A stolen kiss isn't what I want. Look: I'm not even trying to touch the sleeve of your jacket. Don't suppose that I don't understand your reasons for not wanting to let this feeling between us dwindle into an ordinary hole-and-corner love-affair. I couldn't have spoken like this yesterday, because when we've been apart, and I'm looking forward to seeing you, every thought is burnt up in a great flame. But then you come; and you're so much more than I remembered, and what I want of you is so much more than an hour or two every now and then, with wastes of thirsty waiting between, that I can sit perfectly still beside you, like this, with that other vision in my mind, just quietly trusting to it to come true."[12]

For romantic love to emerge, the real person need not be present; what is necessary is the existence of the image. Lacan first defines love in terms of a narcissistic relationship of the subject: what is at work in falling in love is the recognition of the narcissistic image that forms the substance of the ideal ego. When we fall in love, we position the person who is the object of our love in the place of the ideal ego. We love this object because of the perfection we have striven to reach for our own ego. However, it is not only that the subject loves in the other the image he or she would like to inhabit him- or herself. The subject simultaneously posits the object of his or her love in the place of the Ego Ideal, from which the subject would like to see him- or herself in a likeable way. When we are in love, the love object placed in the Ego Ideal enables us to perceive ourselves in a new way – compassionate, lovable, beautiful, decent, etc. Because of the Ideal invested in the person we love, we feel shame in front of her or him or we try to fascinate this person.

However, to understand the mechanisms of love, one has to look beyond the Ideal. Lacan's famous definition of love is that the subject gives to the other what he or she does not have. This object is the traumatic *objet petit a*, the object cause of desire. Behind the narcissistic relationship toward the love-object we encounter the real, the traumatic object in ourselves, as well as in the other: "Analysis demonstrates that love, in its essence, is narcissistic, and reveals that the substance of what is supposedly object-like (*objectal*) – what a bunch of bull – is in fact that which constitutes a remainder in desire, namely, its cause, and sustains desire through its lack of satisfaction (*insatisfaction*), and even its impossibility."[13]

How does the subject relate to the object of his or her desire in romantic love? Newland wants to escape with Ellen to a place where they would be able to freely enjoy their love, where they would be "simply two human beings who love each other; and nothing else on earth will matter". Significantly, it is Newland – the conformist – who believes in the possibility of this place of fulfillment outside institutions, and it is Ellen, the nonconformist half-outcast, who dispels his illusions when she answers him by saying:

> "Oh, my dear – where is that country? Have you ever been there? ... I know of so many who've tried to find it; and, believe me, they all got out by mistake at wayside stations; at places like Boulogne, or Pisa, or Monte-Carlo – and it wasn't at all different from the old world they'd left, but only rather smaller and dingier and more promiscuous ... Ah, believe me, it's a miserable little country!" ...
>
> "Then what, exactly, is your plan for us?" he asked.
>
> "For us? But there is no us in that sense! We're near each other only if we stay far from each other. Then we can be ourselves. Otherwise we're only Newland Archer, the husband of Ellen Olenska's cousin, and Ellen Olenska, the cousin of Newland Archer's wife, trying to be happy behind the backs of the people who trust them."
>
> "Ah, I'm beyond that," he groaned.
>
> "No, you're not! You've never been beyond. And *I* have, and I know what it looks like there."[14]

It is only at the very end of the novel that this message – and thereby the truth of Newland's desire – is brought home to him. Lacan points out that "desire is formed as something ... the demand means beyond whatever it is able to formulate".[15] On the level of *demand*, Newland's passion could be perceived as his wish to unite with Ellen; however, his *desire* is to renounce this unification: Newland submits himself to the social code to maintain Ellen as the inaccessible object that sets his desire in motion. This logic enables us to understand the ending of the novel when Newland, now widowed, decides during his trip to Paris not to see Ellen and thus finally gives up the consummation of his great love. Newland, sitting in front of Ellen's house, tries to imagine what goes on in the apartment:

> "It's more real to me here than if I went up," he suddenly heard himself say; and the fear lest that last shadow of reality should lose its edge kept him rooted to his seat as the minutes succeeded each other.
>
> He sat for a long time on the bench in the thickening dusk, his eyes never turning from the balcony. At length a light shone through the windows, and a moment later a man-servant came out on the balcony, drew up the awnings, and closed the shutters.
>
> At that, as if it had been the signal he waited for, Newland Archer got up slowly and walked back alone to his hotel.[16]

This last act is an ethical one in the Lacanian sense of "not giving up on one's desire". All previous renunciations of the love affair between New-land and Ellen depended on an "ethics with the excuse". Thus we can read Ellen's statement, "I can't love you unless I give you up",[17] as a declaration of romantic love and not as an ethical act: the love becomes romantic because of the suffering it involves. Similarly, Newland's giving up on Ellen in his youth is still linked to the expectation of a "future" when he will stop lying to his wife and when the reality (of his love) will take a true form. Only the last renunciation has the meaning of an ethical act because there is no utilitarian demand any more. From a pragmatic point of view, this renunciation is stupid: Newland is celibate, as is Ellen; he still loves her; presumably she is also far from indifferent to him; even Newland's son wants his father to rediscover his great love. Not only are there no social obstacles to their relationship, it is even Newland's society's expectation that a young widower find a new life companion.

Why did Newland decide not to see Ellen? The answer could be traced in "the fear lest that last shadow of reality should lose its edge". Our perception of reality is linked to the fact that something has to be precluded from it: the object as the point of the gaze. Every screen of reality includes a constitutive "stain", the trace of what had to be precluded from the field of reality in order that this field can acquire its consistency; this stain appears in the guise of a void Lacan names object *a*. It is the point that I, the subject, cannot see: it eludes me insofar as it is the point from which the screen itself "returns the gaze", or watches me, that is, the point where the gaze itself is inscribed into the visual field of reality. For Newland's reality to retain consistency, this object has to stay closed in the room in Paris. That is why he can leave the scene when the man-servant closes the window. This gesture of closing the window is a sign for Newland: a sign that the object is securely precluded so that his reality may remain intact.

Throughout his life, Newland perceived his married life with May as a necessity to which he must submit because society expected it of him, and because of the "innocence" and "purity" of his lovely wife. At the very end of the novel, however, he encounters another duty: the recognition that there is no "other country", that there is no "beyond" the codes and rituals that have suppressed him throughout his life.

The other person who is aware of the lack of any "beyond" is May. After May's death, Newland learns that she knew about his great love for Ellen. However, May responded to this fact in her "innocent" way: she never revealed her knowledge or reproached Newland, but manipulated the situation with the help of the social rules and codes. This recognition of the non-existence of anything "beyond" the institutions is what May paradoxically has in common with Ellen.

THE BIG OTHER IN LOVE

How does it happen that people subordinate themselves to the logic of the institution and obey all kinds of social ritual that are supposedly against their well-being? Althusser points out that individuals, in their relation to other individuals, function in the mode of transference.[18] Transference is thus the "stuff" of social relations. But what is transference other than a specific form of love? What then is the function of love as a social bond?

In his writings on psychoanalysis, Althusser refers to Stendhal's *The Red and the Black*. This novel is an esthetic discourse composed of a series of utterances, presented in a certain order. This discourse is the very existence of Julien and his "passions": Julien's passions in their affective violence do not precede the discourse, nor are they something uttered between the lines – his passion is the discourse itself: "The *constraints* which define this *discourse* are the very existence of this 'passion'."[19] The same goes for the discourse of the unconscious: "the unconscious is structured as language" means that the unconscious is the constraints that are at work in this discourse, that these constraints are the very existence of the unconscious – there is no unconscious hidden behind the discursive constraints that "express" themselves in the discourse.

The effect (of the unconscious, of "passions") is therefore not exterior to the mechanism that produces the effect: "The effect is nothing other than the discourse itself."[20] For each discourse can be said to be defined by a system of specific constraints that function as the law of the language; and the effects of this discourse are the products of the constraints. In the case of the unconscious, the constraints that function in this discourse produce the libido as its effect; in the case of ideological discourse, the constraints produce the effect of (mis)recognition.

Similarly, it is the constraint (of discourse, of the social symbolic structure) that actually produces love. This institution concerns what Lacan names "the big Other". In his seminar on transference, Lacan pointed out the role that the big Other plays in love: "the divine place of the Other" consecrates the relationship between subjects, as long as the providence of the desire of the loved one inscribes itself in this divine place.[21]

In Lacanian psychoanalysis, the Other is a symbolic structure in which the subject has always been embedded. This symbolic structure is not a positive social fact: it is quasi-transcendental, and forms the frame structuring our perception of reality; its status is normative, it is a world of symbolic rules and codes. As such, it also does not belong to the psychic level: it is a radically external, non-psychological universe of symbolic codes regulating our psychic self-experience. It is a mistake either to internalize the big Other and reduce it to a psychological fact, or to externalize the big Other and reduce it to institutions in social reality. By doing either, we miss the fact that language is in itself an institution to which the subject is submitted.

How is love connected to the big Other? There is no love outside speech: non-speaking beings do not love. As La Rochefoucauld observed, people do not love if they do not speak about it. Love emerges out of speech as a demand that is not linked to any need. Love is a demand that constitutes itself as such only because the subject is the subject of the signifier.[22] As such, the subject is split, barred, marked by a fundamental lack. And it is in this lack that one encounters the object cause of desire. This object has a paradoxical status: it is what the subject lacks, and at the same time what fills this lack. The enchantment of love is how the subject deals, on the one hand, with his or her own lack, and, on the other hand, with the lack in the loved one. As such, love does not call for an answer, although we usually think it does: "Since men have been writing about love, it is clear that they survived far better the longer the beauty remained mute, the longer she did not answer at all – which provokes the thought that the discourse on love itself engenders a kind of *jouissance*, that it makes the extreme limit at which speech becomes *jouissance*, a *jouissance* of the speech itself."[23]

The fact that love does not expect an answer can be understood as bearing witness to its imaginary, narcissistic character: any possible answer from the beloved object would undermine this narcissistic relationship and disturb the mirroring of the subject's ego in the beloved object. In the case of *The Remains of the Day*, for example, Miss Kenton does not expect Stevens's answer, she actually seeks to escape from the possible answer. Her act of marriage is a kind of acting out that tried to resolve the dilemma of her love for Stevens. However, her intention was not to hear a confession of Stevens's love for her: for a hysteric, the world collapses if the master loses his sacred place and becomes human.

However, the perception of love as a narcissistic relation loses ground the moment we take into account that "love is a demand (although it remains without the answer) that addresses being . . . some being that is inaccessible as long as it does not answer. Love addresses that point in speech where the word fails. Confronted with this experience, the subject has two solutions at hand: he can either try to encircle the point where he no longer has any words, or to stuff it with a stopper."[24] What love as a demand targets in the other is therefore the object in him- or herself, the real, non-symbolizable kernel around which the subject organizes his or her desire. What gives the beloved his or her dignity, what leads the loving subject to the survalorization of the beloved, is the presence of the object in him or her:

> by being overvalued, it [the object] has the task of saving the dignity of the subject, that is, of making something else out of us than a subject submitted to the endless sliding of the signifier. It makes of us something other from the subject of speech, and exactly this something other is unique, invaluable, irreplaceable, it is the true point at which we can finally mark what I have named the dignity of the subject.[25]

As we have already seen, the subject can relate to this object in two ways. On the one hand, he or she can use the object as the stopper which, by its fascinating and *éblouissante* presence, renders invisible the lack in the Other: as is the case in the elevation of the object in romantic love. On the other hand, the subject can deal with the object in terms of sublimation, of a circulation around the object that never touches its core. Sublimation is not a form of romantic love kept alive by the endless striving for the inaccessible love-object. In sublimation, the subject confronts the horrifying dimension of the object, the object as *das Ding*, the traumatic foreign body in the symbolic structure. Sublimation circles around the object; it is driven by the fact that the object can never be reached because of its impossible, horrifying nature. Whereas romantic love strives to enjoy the whole of the Other, of the partner, true sublime love renounces, since it is well aware that we can "only enjoy a part of the Other's body . . . That is why we must confine ourselves to simply giving it a little squeeze, like that, taking a forearm or anything else – ouch!"[26]

Such sublimation is well exemplified in Jane Campion's film *The Piano*. What I have in mind here is not only the slow advance of the two lovers to the sexual act, their endless foreplay in which the body of the other is accessible only part by part and never as a whole (the little piece of skin that can be reached through the hole in Holly Hunter's stocking, for example), but the contractual relationship that exists between the characters played by Harvey Keitel and Holly Hunter. The two make a deal in which she can earn back her piano by allowing Keitel to touch her. This contract is so specific that it even defines how many piano keys are worth a certain touch. The miracle is that out of this subordination to the sexual contract the most passionate and sublime love emerges.

A similar development is at work in Pedro Almódovar's film *Átame* (*Tie me up, tie me down*), in which the kidnapper ties up the actress but never sexually abuses her: their daily ritual unexpectedly produces love – the actress falls in love with her kidnapper and even plans to marry him. Here, the partial discovery of the body of the loved one takes place through the act of tying: when the kidnapper carefully chooses the appropriate knot or when he buys masking tape that allows the actress to breathe, he discovers her body part by part. The kidnapper does not do what might be expected, he does not take the actress by force, he does not try to take her "whole". Through the ritual of tying he remains always distanced and thus ignites her desire for him.

This, then, is the supreme paradox of love and institution: true sublime love can only emerge against the background of an external, contractual, symbolic exchange mediated by the institution. Love is not only the guise for the impossibility of relationship with fellow beings, but also the dissimulation that covers the subject's own radical lack. Freud's maxim, "love for oneself knows only one barrier – love for others, love for objects", can thus be paraphrased as: "love for others knows only one barrier – love for oneself, love for the object in oneself".

"NEVER, WILL I STOOP TO WANTING ANYTHING ELSE"

The way the subject deals with his or her radical lack could also be the cause of his or her constant failure in love relationships. One encounters such a failure in a hysteric who desperately searches for the Other who would eternally love her and thus annihilate her radical lack.

One example of this attitude is found in Edith Wharton's "The Muse's Tragedy". In this short story we encounter two unrealized love relation-ships, first between the famous poet Vincent Rendle and a married lady, Mrs. Anerton, and second, between Mrs. Anerton and a young writer, Lewis Danyers. Here is a summary of the story: Danyers is a great admirer of the late poet Vincent Rendle and has written an excellent article about his work. One of the most distinguished of Rendle's works is the "Sonnets to Silvia". Widespread rumor has it that Silvia is actually Mrs. Anerton, with whom Rendle presumably had a secret love affair. Danyers has a strong desire to meet this woman who had been such an inspiration for the famous poet. Once, during a vacation in Italy, Danyers happens to run into Mrs. Anerton, who is now widowed, living a lonely life. Through their long conversations about Rendle's poetry, Danyers and Mrs. Anerton quickly become close friends. At the end of the holiday, they decide to meet again in a month, ostensibly so that Danyers can start writing a book on Rendle with her help. However, this project is more an excuse for them to see each other again. The last part of the story consists of a long letter from Mrs. Anerton to Danyers, in which we discover that when they met again in Venice, they had a wonderful time, not once mentioning the dead poet. At the end of their stay, Danyers had asked Mrs. Anerton to marry him, and in this letter she explains why she cannot accept his offer. Mrs. Anerton confesses that, contrary to widespread belief, there was never anything but friendship between her and Rendle; she was never Rendle's lover, although she had been very much in love with him. Since she never was Silvia, the object of Rendle's love, she cannot accept Danyers's proposal; although she is very much taken by him, Danyers cannot take the place of the unattainable love-object that Rendle was.

What is common to all the protagonists of the story is their love for poetry: they are either poets or close readers of poetry. But poetry, through its own elusive character, also represents the object of love. In a poem, rhythm and form capture that "something more" that makes a poem a work of art, an artistic object that is also an object in a Lacanian sense of the term: an object that has no price, an object that is at the same time both beautiful and horrifying and that sets our desire in motion. Like the art object, the object of love is framed. Mrs. Anerton, for example, was described to Danyers as being like "one of those old prints where the lines have the value of color".[27] For Danyers, the "Sonnets to Silvia" were the frame into which Mrs. Anerton was placed as the object of his desire, long before he met her. Symptomatically, Mrs. Anerton becomes the object of Danyers's love in the first instance because he assumes that she was the great love of the famous poet. At work here is the Lacanian maxim that desire is always the desire of the Other.[28]

The first meaning of this maxim is that the subject desires the same thing as the Other, either in the sense of a concrete other human being or in the sense of the symbolic order. For Danyers, Rendle, the most admired poet of his time, was the Other in whom he invested his Ego Ideal; thus Danyers became fascinated by the woman who was supposedly the object of Rendle's love. Notably, when Danyers "really" falls in love with Mrs. Anerton, the dead poet quickly becomes an intruder, since now Danyers himself wants to become the object of Mrs. Anerton's love. This shows the second meaning of the maxim "desire is the desire of the Other", which concerns the subject's question as to what kind of an object he or she is for the Other. It is significant that Danyers never questions whether he loves Mrs. Anerton as herself, or only as Rendle's assumed mistress. When Danyers falls in love, the essential thing for him is what *he* represents in the eyes of Mrs. Anerton. That is why he is so flattered when she inquires about his work and encourages him to start writing again:

"You must write," she said, administering the most exquisite flattery that human lips could give.

Of course he meant to write – why not do something great in his turn? His best, at least; with the resolve, at the outset, that his should be *the* best. Nothing less seemed possible with that mandate in his ears. How she had divined him; lifted and disentangled his groping ambitions; laid the awakening touch on his spirit with her creative *Let there be light!*[29]

This quotation offers a perfect example of the Freudian description of love as a narcissistic relationship: the subject posits the object of his or her love in the place of the Ego Ideal and then tries to appear before this object in the most lovable way, as the most admirable human being. This positing reflects the lover's desire that the beloved return love and thus subjectify himself or herself as a lover, too. The reason Danyers is so fascinated by Mrs. Anerton's encouragement to write is that this encouragement proves to him that she sees in him that "something more" – the artistic genius, the object of her admiration, a possible love. Mrs. Anerton's urging him to write gives Danyers hope that the "something more" that he sees in her she acknowledges in him, too, and that, therefore, love is reciprocal. His enthusiasm is quickly shattered when Mrs. Anerton proposes to Danyers that he write a book on Rendle: with this proposal, Danyers loses the place of the object of Mrs. Anerton's love, and becomes merely the link to Mrs. Anerton's love for the dead poet. From the letter we can guess that this situation changes when they meet in Venice and that at this time Rendle's spirit ceases to haunt them, which encourages Danyers to ask Mrs. Anerton for her hand.

Danyers presents a fairly simple scheme of love: a man becomes fascinated with his Ideal, and when this Ideal apparently returns love (when the spirit of the dead poet presumably leaves the stage) the realization of a love relationship in marriage seems the natural course of events. But with Mrs. Anerton things are more complicated.

Her relationship with Rendle was an intellectual friendship between equals. From her description of the relationship, it is clear that Rendle treated her as an intellectual partner, as a friend who knew a lot about poetry and as a person with whom he could have interesting conversations. As Mrs. Anerton writes:

"He was always quite honest and straightforward with me; he treated me as one man treats another; and yet at times I felt he *must* see that with me it was different. If he did see, he made no sign. Perhaps he never noticed – I am sure he never meant to be cruel. He had never made love to me; it was no fault of his if I wanted more than he could give me."[30]

We also learn from Mrs. Anerton's letter to Danyers that the famous "Sonnets to Silvia" were written as a "cosmic philosophy" and not as a love poem: they were addressed to Woman and not to a woman. After Rendle's death, when Mrs. Anerton edited a book of his letters, she slightly changed the letters that Rendle had addressed to her by marking them at certain points to indicate that something had been left out, thus giving the impression to the reader that the more intimate parts were held back from publication. Although the "Sonnets to Silvia" were addressed to a non-existing Woman, Mrs. Anerton did all she could to maintain the impression that in reality she was Silvia. Mrs. Anerton thus identified with Woman. What is the logic of such an identification?

Lacanian theory maintains that Woman does not exist. Lacan points out that no general notion of Woman can embrace all women. Woman is for men, as for women, barred, crossed, just as the big Other is also barred: Woman is radically unattainable, "what women never are by themselves, a woman that is mythologized as ideal, muse, etc.".[31] The belief in Woman is therefore nothing other than an attempt to erase the bar that marks the subject and to negate the lack in the Other. That is why, for Lacan, Woman is essentially a man's fantasy. This mythical woman, a muse or an ideal, is in itself asexual. And the identification with this ideal presents an attempt to escape the split, the lack that pertains to the sexual difference.

Such a desperate attempt to identify with Woman arises in the transsexual's demand for a change of sex. As Catherine Millot[32] points out in her analysis of transsexualism, transsexual men usually identify with Woman (La femme) when they demand the operation that would change their sex. With this demand, male transsexuals put the image of Woman in the place of the Name-of-the-Father in an attempt to escape castration. A transsexual man tries to be more feminine than a woman, which is why he tries to embody "all women". In this attempt, the transsexual man falls prey to the male myth that presupposes the existence of Woman as the being not submitted to castration. As someone who is not castrated, Woman serves the same function as the Freudian primordial father who, as the possessor of all the women, also possesses all jouissance and thus blocks his sons' access to their jouissance. Lacan points out that "Woman is one of the Names-of-the-Father".[33] But as Millot says, for the transsexual, Woman occupies the place of the Name-of-the-Father. Here, as Jacques-Alain Miller emphasizes, one has to be careful to distinguish the Name-of-the-Father from the Names-of-the-Father: the first notion delineates the empty form of the law, the father as the symbolic function, while the plural of the Name-of-the-Father means the Freudian primordial father, the father who is the full embodiment of authority and not the empty symbolic figure.[34] Woman therefore does not play the role of the empty symbolic father, but as one of the Names-of-the-Father occupies the place of the primordial father. According to Catherine Millot, transsexuals do not present a case of psychosis, even though the Name-of-the-Father is missing, since "the transsexual symptom *strictu sensu* (conviction and the demand for transformation) corresponds to an attempt to palliate the absence of the Name-of-the-Father ... The transsexual symptom appears to function as a substitution of the Name-of-the-Father inasmuch as the transsexual aims to incarnate Woman."[35] This symptom thus performs the paradoxical function of limiting *jouissance* of the subject. Here we find the same logic at work as in the case of the psychotic, who also finds a kind of solution to his or her problems by forming a delirium. Such a delirium or symptom allows some psychotics to posit a limit to *jouissance*. Lacan argued that, in the case of James Joyce, his writing was the symptom that replaced the missing function of the Name-of-the-Father and thus prevented Joyce from falling into actual psychosis.[36] Likewise, in the case of transsexuals, their symptom (the demand to incarnate Woman) replaces the Name-of-the-Father and thus also prevents psychosis.

What happens if a woman identifies with Woman? She also has two possibilities: psychosis and hysteria. In hysterical identification with Woman, the paternal function, the Name-of-the-Father, is fully in place: however, the hysteric is traumatized by the split that pertains to her entry into language, and to escape this split, she tries to present herself as a phallic Woman.

As was pointed out in the discussion of *The Remains of the Day*, the hysteric is perturbed by the question "what am I for the Other?" The hysteric does not try to obtain the satisfaction of her desire through this question, but to question the desire of the Other, since for the hysteric, the problem is that she encounters her desire as Other. Thus the trauma of the hysteric evolves around the dilemma of what kind of object she is for the Other without knowing it. The hysteric's question in regard to love is thus not "Do I love him?" but a narcissistic "Does he love me?" The narcissism of the subject found in hysteria is a fundamental narcissism that touches the very core of the subject's being. The hysteric's narcissism is linked to her desperate attempt for certainty: what she seeks is the Other who would grant her identity. The hysteric's questions and appeals to the Other to tell her who she is, what value she has and what object she is, are all attempts to overcome the constitutive split that marks the subject as a speaking being. The hysteric searches for the signifier that would give her unity, wholeness: "In the meantime, she becomes devoted to the cult of Woman . . . in the hope that this signifier will someday appear."[37]

Hysteria is also the subject's way of dealing with the impossibility of sexual rapport. The hysteric's symptoms are usually desperate attempts to deny this impossibility. In his scheme of the discourse of the hysteric, Lacan points out how the hysteric tries to overcome the impossibility of sexual rapport via the belief that the Other has knowledge about her (that the Other knows the truth about her object *a*); thus she believes that such an Other exists and that it is flawless. The hysteric also demands that every man be the embodiment of this Other, which forces her to constantly question the authority of her partner. "The hysteric, looking for an Other without lack, offers herself to him as phallicized object to make him complete, to install him as Other without flaw."[38] With this desperate attempt, the hysteric hopes to become the only object of the desire of the Other, which would give her certainty about her being.[39]

How are we to understand the hysteric's attempt to embody the phallus? For Lacan, the phallus occupies the position of the third element that disrupts the symbiosis between subjects. In the relationship between the mother and the child, the father's phallus is what prevents the child from being all for the mother, i.e. mother does not desire only her child (the child is not all for her) because of the phallus. What is crucial is that "the phallus forbids the child the satisfaction of his or her own desire, which is the desire to be the exclusive desire of the mother".[40] The phallus is a signifier of the desire of the Other and, as such, it is a signifier equivalent to the lack in the Other. For Lacan, the phallus marks the entry of the subject into language, since it introduces the child to symbolic castration: "Castration means first of all this – that the child's desire for the mother does not refer *to* her but *beyond* her, to an object, the phallus, whose status is first imaginary (the object presumed to satisfy her desire) and then symbolic (recognition that desire cannot be satisfied)."[41]

Of women who deal with the trauma of castration by attempting to be the phallus, Lacan says: "Paradoxical as this formulation may seem, I am saying that it is in order to be the phallus, that is to say, the signifier of the desire of the Other, that a woman will reject an essential part of femininity, namely, all her attributes in the masquerade. It is for that which she is not that she wishes to be desired as well as loved."[42] Lacan took the term masquerade from Joan Riviere, for whom womanliness is a masquerade that is at the same time a dissimulation of a certain masculinity, a mask a woman puts on in order to incite man's desire, a mask that presents horror for men, since men suspect some hidden danger behind it. This masquerade for Lacan concerns the phallus, which is primarily a fraud, a semblance, nothing in itself, only a signifier of the lack as such – "the supreme signifier of an impossible identity".[43]

What is at stake in Mrs. Anerton's love life is not so much her desiring an unattainable love object (Rendle) but her identifying with the object that is presumably desired by Rendle. She masquerades as a phallic Woman – Silvia, since it is Silvia that is the signifier of Rendle's desire. Silvia is the object of his desire that goes beyond any existing woman, which is why she can take on the role of the phallus. In this desperate attempt to be the object of Rendle's love, Mrs. Anerton did everything to maintain the public impression that she was Silvia. But, although she desperately tried to identify with Woman, to be Silvia, Rendle's muse, she always knew that this project was doomed to failure. As she says in her letter to Danyers, for moments she would almost believe that she was Silvia because of the rumors people were spreading, but she knew this was not true: "Oh, there was no phase of folly I didn't go through. You can't imagine the excuses a woman will invent for a man's not telling her that he loves her . . . But all the while, deep down, I knew he had never cared."[44] And because of this awareness, Mrs. Anerton was not a psychotic but a hysteric. She *would* be a psychotic had she never doubted that she *was* Silvia. In that case, she would not have needed to encourage rumors about her being Rendle's love. However, because Mrs. Anerton did not truly identify herself as Silvia, she needed symbolic structures (rumors, the published letters that she herself edited, etc.) through which she could organize a whole fantasy scenario that would assure others, and through their belief assure herself, that she was Silvia.

Eric Laurent says that there are many women who, in the name of love, "try to give all and be all" – and thus try to embody the non-existent fantasy of Woman. When women recognize the impossibility of such an attitude, they usually fall into the other extreme and start perceiving themselves as nothing. "The wrong solution given by female masochism is that the subject tries to reserve for herself the place in man's fantasy that would be all or nothing. This solution is wrong since the reality of woman's position for man is not to be all or nothing, but to be his Other."[45] To be all, to be "the Woman all men are missing", therefore involves a psychotic stance. In this case, Woman becomes "the Other of the Other", which is a psychotic position because it has no representation in the symbolic.[46]

The pathos of Mrs. Anerton is that she tried to get proof that she was not this "nothing", not someone unworthy of love, in her relationship with Danyers. As she admits in the letter, her original aim was to provoke Danyers's love to get reassurance of her own worth. However, she miscalculated the course of the events that followed, since she herself started feeling for Danyers more than she intended. That her feelings for Danyers were more than cunning cordiality becomes clear at the end of her letter, when she worries whether Danyers was sincere in his feelings: did he intend only to play around with her; did he love her as Silvia or as herself? These are again a hysteric's questions, through which Mrs. Anerton tries to learn what kind of an object she is for Danyers.

When the hysteric subject poses the question of his or her being, of what he or she is for the Other, the subject does not get an answer. The Other does not answer. Thus the subject tries to obtain proof outside words: in acts, behavior, between the lines, etc. The subject thus becomes an interpreter. Since the Other cannot answer, the subject invents the answer to the question of the Other's desire.[47] Mrs. Anerton admits to Danyers that there was one question that hounded her night and day, that became her obsession: "Why had he [Rendle] never loved me? Why had I been so much to him, and no more? Was I so ugly, so essentially unlovable, that though a man might cherish me as his mind's comrade, he could not care for me as a woman?"[48] Her experiment with Danyers was supposed to tell her who she was as a woman, to affirm her ability to be an object of love. However, as she says in the letter, she did not plan it all: "I liked you from the first – I was drawn to you (you must have seen that) – I wanted you to like me; it was not a mere psychological experiment."[49] That Mrs. Anerton cared for Danyers more than she initially intended is noticeable from her joy in recognizing how jealous Danyers is of her past. Further evidence of her interest in Danyers emerges when Mrs. Anerton explains why she did not reject him earlier during their stay in Venice: "I couldn't spoil that month – my one month. It was so good, for once in my life, to get away from literature."[50] Her desperate attempt to identify with Silvia accounted for the fact that in her past there was no love for Mrs. Anerton outside literature; but by meeting Danyers she got a glimpse of what "true" love could be: when she and Danyers escaped the grip of the dead poet, they opened a space for a genuine love to begin.

But why did Mrs. Anerton prevent this from happening? The answer is not that she still loved the dead poet and did not want to give up on her desire for him. From what Mrs. Anerton says in the letter, it could be concluded that her refusal of Danyers has something to do with how her relationship with him uncovers the falsehood of the story that she had created about her relationship with Rendle and her complete, if not fatal, belief in that story. When Mrs. Anerton recognizes the full scope of the illusion in which she has lived for most of her life, her whole identity collapses. As she speculates at the end of the letter, being a young man, Danyers will probably quickly forget the pain that she has caused him, but her experiment will affect her far more deeply: "it will hurt me horribly . . ., because it has shown me, for the first time, all that I have missed".[51] However, Mrs. Anerton's refusal of Danyers can also be understood as another hysterical gesture. Her refusal of love has to do with the impossibility of her desire. What she was primarily concerned with in both of her failed love relationships was: what kind of an object is she for the Other, first for Rendle and then for Danyers? It was also in her relationship with Danyers that her primal concern evolved around her demand to be the object of his love. Danyers's actual falling in love with her would mean the fulfillment of her desire. However, this is what the hysteric cannot accept: her desire has to remain unsatisfied. But in this refusal, she presents her act as an act of assisting Danyers. As she says in the letter: "Somebody must save you from marrying a disappointed woman."[52]

In giving up Danyers, does Mrs. Anerton act in a Socratic way by revealing the truth that she is not Silvia? Does she, in effect, admit to her lover, "there where you see something, I am nothing". As Lacan stresses in his analysis of Plato's *Symposium*, Socrates refuses Alcibiades' courting and does not recognize himself as the loved one because "for [Socrates] there is nothing in himself worthy of love. His essence was that *ouden*, emptiness, hollowness."[53] Socrates' refusal to acknowledge himself as the loved one and to return love discloses the traumatic, empty nature of the object of love. As Lacan says, "the Other whom we long for is anything other than love, it is something that literally causes the love to decay – I want to say, something that has the nature of an object".[54] When Socrates refuses to be the object worthy of Alcibiades' desire, he reveals that the object of love does not possess what the loving one expects.[55] Mrs. Anerton does not act in the Socratic tradition, since she still believes in that "something more" in her that should be worthy of love. That is why she can write: "It is just when a man begins to think that he understands a woman that he may be sure that he doesn't. It is because Vincent Rendle *didn't love me* that there is no hope for you. I never had what I wanted, and never, never, never, will I stoop to wanting anything else."[56]

How then are we to understand Mrs. Anerton's giving up on Danyers when, on the one hand, it is clear from her letter that she was truly happy with him, but, on the other hand, her nostalgia for her unconsumated love with Rendle remains constant. Mrs. Anerton falls into the paradox of love when she expects from it something other than what is at work in it. A common question among loved women is: does the man love me for myself or for something else? In a film by Claude Chabrol, the hero, a millionaire, reverses the logic of this question by saying: "I do not want a woman who will love me for myself. Finally I would like to meet one that will love me for my millions." However absurd it might sound, this "reversed logic" represents the true nature of love. The expectation that the other will love you for yourself is some kind of a psychotic position: in this case, the loved one takes him- or herself as the subject without lack. The truth about love is that the other has to love you for something that is in you more than yourself.

Until their meeting in Venice, Danyers obviously loved Mrs. Anerton because she seemed to be the object of the desire of the Other (Rendle). However, he did not recognize the moment when he started to love her regardless of her relationship with Rendle. In Danyers's libidinal economy, his love for Mrs. Anerton was always the love for that "something more than herself". Mrs. Anerton, in contrast, had an impossible demand: she wanted Danyers to love her both as what she was herself and as something else, as Silvia, the phantasmatic muse. This impossible demand reflects the impossibility of the sexual relationship; for Mrs. Anerton, her relationship with Danyers collapsed when the image of Silvia faded and when the Other, Rendle, disappeared from her unity with Danyers. The relationship between Danyers and Mrs. Anerton might have been possible had Mrs. Anerton still presumed that Danyers loved her as Silvia. However, Mrs. Anerton would really have had to have been Silvia (her love for Rendle would have had to be realized).

Mrs. Anerton came close to an understanding of what love is when she falsified Rendle's published letters by inserting asterisks to signify the omission of passages that were never there in the first place. This lack is the object of love. However, her tragedy is that she wants this emptiness to be fullness and to have a name – Silvia. Mrs. Anerton therefore wants to be all, the full object of love, and when she realizes that she is not, she rejects love altogether and chooses nothingness. She can not deal with the fact that she is lacking as a subject; since she cannot accept love's phantasmatic nature, and since she did not realize her grandest love, Mrs. Anerton also gives up on her second chance of love.

Paradoxically this is the limit of love – that we see in the other what he or she does not have, and not him- or herself. This is the very condition of love. The position of the hysterical subject is to always have to guess what is behind the curtain, which is why such a subject usually ends up having nothing – by totally giving up on love.

The subjects in *The Age of Innocence* and *The Remains of the Day* needed the big Other (society's codes, institutions) to prevent their love from being realized, but Mrs. Anerton creates her own prohibitions by constantly seeking the way to be Woman, the Muse[57] that would be the true object of the Other's desire. And by not recognizing the emptiness of this object, she gives up on love. While a poet longs for the object of his love, his Muse, and creates around this impossible object a work of art, the Muse must live in the realm of disavowal.

NOTES

1. Sigmund Freud, *Sexuality and the Psychology of Love*, New York: Macmillan 1963, p. 57.
2. Louis Althusser, *Lenin and Philosophy and Other Essays*, London: New Left Books 1971, p. 136.
3. Kazuo Ishiguro, *The Remains of the Day*, London: Faber and Faber 1989, pp. 9–10.
4. Stuart Schneiderman, *Rat Man*, New York: New York University Press 1986, p. 35.
5. Sigmund Freud, "Notes upon a case of obsessional neurosis (The 'Rat Man')", *Standard Edition*, Vol. X, p. 245.
6. Ishiguro, *The Remains of the Day*, p. 131.
7. Ibid.
8. Ibid., p. 42.

9. Ibid., p. 169.
10. Jacques-Alain Miller, "Sur le Gide de Lacan", *La Cause Freudienne* 25 (1993), p. 37.
11. Significantly, Stevens points out that butlers truly exist only in England. In other countries they have only men-servants: "Continentals are unable to be butlers because they are as a breed incapable of the emotional restraint which only the English race are capable of." Ishiguro, *The Remains of the Day*, p. 43.
12. Edith Wharton, *The Age of Innocence*, New York: Macmillan 1986, p. 289.
13. Jacques Lacan, *On Feminine Sexuality: The Limits of Love and Knowledge (Book XX – Encore 1972–1973)*, trans. Bruce Fink, New York: Norton 1998, p. 6.
14. Wharton, *The Age of Innocence*, pp. 290, 291.
15. Jacques Lacan, *The Ethics of Psychoanalysis* (1959–60), London: Routledge 1992, p. 294.
16. Wharton, *The Age of Innocence*, p. 362.
17. Ibid., p. 172.
18. Louis Althusser, *Ecrits sur la psychanalyse: Freud et Lacan*, Paris: Stock/Imec 1993, p. 176.
19. Ibid., p. 157.
20. Ibid., p. 158.
21. See Jacques Lacan, *Le Séminaire, livre VIII: Le transfert*, Paris: Editions du Seuil 1991.
22. See Jacques Lacan, *Ecrits: A Selection*, trans. Alan Sheridan, New York: Norton 1977, p. 270.
23. Michel Silvestre, *Demain la psychanalyse*, Paris: Navarin Editeur 1987, pp. 300–301.
24. Ibid., p. 301.
25. Lacan, *Le Séminaire, livre VIII: Le transfert*, p. 203.
26. Lacan, *On Feminine Sexuality*, p. 23.
27. Edith Wharton, "The Muse's Tragedy", in *Souls Belated and Other Stories*, London: Everyman 1991, p. 29.
28. See Jacques Lacan, "The Subversion of the Subject and the Dialectic of Desire in the Freudian Unconscious", in *Ecrits: A Selection*, p. 312.
29. Wharton, "The Muse's Tragedy", p. 35.
30. Ibid., p. 38.
31. Elizabeth Cowie, *To Represent Woman? The Representation of Sexual Difference in the Visual Media*, London: Macmillan 1997, p. 205.
32. See Catherine Millot, *Horsexe: Essay on Transsexuality*, New York: Autonomedia 1990.
33. Jacques Lacan, *Le Sinthome*, unpublished seminar (1975–76).
34. Jacques-Alain Miller, *Ce qui fait insigne*, unpublished seminar (1986–87).

35. Millot, *Horsexe*, p. 42.
36. Lacan, *Le Sinthome* (1975–76).
37. Julien Quackleben et al., "Hysterical Discourse", in *Lacanian Theory of Discourse: Subject, Structure and Society*, ed. Mark Bracher, Marshal W. Alcorn, Ronald J. Corthell and Françoise Massardier-Kenney, New York: New York University Press 1994, p. 131.
38. Ibid., p. 136.
39. Concerning the status of hysteria today, see Elisabeth Bronfen, *The Knotted Subject*, Princeton, NJ: Princeton University Press 1998.
40. Jacques Lacan, *Les Formations de l'inconscient*, unpublished seminar (1957–58), quoted by Jacqueline Rose, "Introduction II", in *Feminine Sexuality: Jacques Lacan and the Ecole Freudienne*, ed. Juliet Mitchell and Jacqueline Rose, London: Macmillan 1982, p. 38.
41. Rose, "Introduction II", p. 38.
42. Lacan, *Ecrits: A Selection*, p. 290.
43. Stephen Heath, "Joan Riviere and the Masquerade", in *Formations of Fantasy*, ed. Victor Burgin, James Donald and Cora Kaplan, London: Methuen 1986, p. 58.
44. Wharton, "The Muse's Tragedy", p. 38.
45. Eric Laurent, "Positions féminines de l'être", *La Cause Freudienne* 24 (1993), p. 108.
46. Ibid., p. 109.
47. It is the fantasy that gives the subject the answer to the question of desire. What is crucial is that the fantasy is the invention of the subject and not of the Other. Lacan says that desire is the desire of the Other, which means that the subject always determines his or her desire in relation to the Other's desire: it is the presumed Other's desire that keeps the subject's desire in motion. But fantasy is always the fantasy of the subject, the Other does not form fantasies, since the Other does not exist.
48. Wharton, "The Muse's Tragedy", p. 40.
49. Ibid., p. 41.
50. Ibid., p. 42.
51. Ibid.
52. Ibid.
53. Lacan, *Le Séminaire, livre VIII: Le transfert*, p. 185. Does Socrates act in a way similar to the Lady in courtly love who also constantly refuses to return love? It can be said that both, Socrates and the Lady, occupy the same place – both are objects of unfulfilled love. However, the function that they perform in this place is different. The Lady is the master that constantly imposes on her admirer new duties and keeps him on a string by hinting that sometime in the future she might show him some mercy. Socrates, on the contrary, refuses this position of the master. Socrates' refusal points to the emptiness of the object of love, while the Lady believes

that there is in herself something worthy of love. That is why she puts herself in the position of the master (S_1), from which she capriciously gives orders. But Socrates opposes such an attitude altogether and does not want to encourage false hope.

54. Ibid., p. 203.
55. Chapter 2 below shows how Socrates' position is similar to that of the analyst, since both of them occupy the position of the object *a* and try to "keep that nothingness", that emptiness, the traumatic and horrifying nature of the object.
56. Wharton, "The Muse's Tragedy", p. 36.
57. Mrs. Anerton wanted to be – but in reality wasn't – Rendle's Muse. It can be said that, as the object of Danyers's fascination, she was his Muse all the time. The Muse's tragedy was therefore that she was a Muse for the wrong poet.

2

LOVE BETWEEN DESIRE
AND DRIVE

What attracts us in another human being? What actually causes the subject to fall in love? I will deal with this question by taking examples of women and men whose love life is mediated by their passionate attachment to artistic professions like playing music or performing ballet. The competition between love and art has been widely presented in forties and fifties melodramas. I will first focus on two less well-known melodramas, *Rhapsody* (Charles Vidor, 1954) and *The Seventh Veil* (Compton Bennett, 1945), to develop the connections among love, desire and drive in Lacanian psychoanalysis. Reference to *The Red Shoes* (Michael Powell and Emeric Pressburger, 1948) and *Humoresque* (John Negulesco, 1946) will help me to clarify how sexual difference inscribes itself in the context of love and art, i.e. how women and men deal differently with their passionate attachments to their love-objects and to their artistic professions.

RHAPSODY, OR, LOVE AS NARCISSISM

The film starts with the young, rich Lulu, played by Elizabeth Taylor. She accompanies her poor boyfriend Paul (Vittorio Gassman) to Zürich, where he has come to study the violin. Lulu quickly realizes that her lover's first devotion is to music and that his love for her comes second. For this reason, they end their relationship after his very successful first concert. Lulu then marries a pianist, James, who, in his love for Lulu, gives up his career; however, as a result, he starts drinking, and Lulu comes to despise him. In Paris, Lulu once again meets Paul, whom she still loves, and he blames her for ruining James. To become worthy of Paul's love, Lulu decides to help James to continue with his study of music: she devotes herself to his career and forces him to practice. Before James's first concert, Lulu informs him that now that he has become a great pianist, she is going to abandon him for Paul. Heartbroken, James gives the concert in great pain, but he does not give up – the concert is a great success. Lulu listens from the back row and is totally taken by James's performance. Paul waits for her, but she decides that she is not going with him, because she truly loves James.

The plot of this melodrama revolves around the problem of the subject who is never loved in the way he or she would like to be. Both men, Paul and James, love Lulu in a way that she does not want to be loved. Thus, initially it seems that Paul loves her too little and James too much. But Lulu also loves her men in the wrong way: in her love for Paul, she can allow no place for his devotion to music; and James she initially does not love, wanting only his submission to her so she can despise him for it. The paradox of the film is that Lulu starts loving James only at the moment when he is able to forget her and give himself to his music.

In this film, love first seems to concern the subject's narcissistic satisfaction. As was shown in Chapter 1, the subject who takes the object of love as his or her Ego Ideal tries to figure out if he or she appears likeable from the point of view of this Ideal. The subject thus strives to have the loved subject return love so that they can form a harmonious union. Here, the loved one's devotion to something outside the relationship is supposed to prevent the true harmony of love. In the film, music is perceived as what dissolves the love relationship of Lulu and Paul. Lulu thus regards music as a competitor that takes Paul away from her. But paradoxically, in her relationship with James, she wants music to become that for which *he* would be willing to sacrifice everything.

When Lulu is Paul's girlfriend, music is something she simply has to endure; she must take it into account for the sake of love.[1] Paul's triumphant concert marks the moment when she thinks that the compromises are now over and Paul will finally be hers. But Paul and Lulu split up when it becomes clear that his success means only more sacrifices. Lulu's narcissism is hurt: she realizes that she will constantly play second fiddle in his life.

The narcissistic pleasure that Lulu takes from Paul's devotion to music is most visible at the beginning of his concert, where Lulu sits in the front row next to her elderly landlady. During the concert, the camera circulates among the protagonists of the story, showing their expressions and their responses to the music. We see self-confident Paul, entranced by his own performance; the conductor observes him with cold respect; the professor

Figure 1 Paul performs confidently in his first concert.

has an enthusiastic expression; and James looks envious (Figure 1). But essential are the gazes of the two women. Lulu first expresses pride and admiration, but this soon turns into boredom, since she is not fascinated by the beauty of the music, but by Paul's success and her role in his achievement. Thus, we see her coquettishly adjusting her evening wrap to bare a shoulder and observing the reaction of the audience to Paul's playing. The elderly lady next to her, in contrast, observes Paul with a motherly gaze: for her the audience does not exist, since she is exclusively devoted to the performer and the beautiful tones of his music (Figure 2). However, Lulu's narcissistic pleasure quickly ends when, after the concert, Paul pays no attention to her, being more concerned with plans for future concerts.

A different exchange of gazes occurs at the end of the film, at James's concert. James, in contrast to self-confident Paul, desperately looks in the direction of the audience, observing the empty seat in the front row where

Figure 2 Lulu observes Paul on stage.

Lulu was supposed to sit. His playing is full of pain and fear. The gazes of the professor and the conductor also express anxiety (Figure 3). The camera then moves to the back row, where Lulu observes the performance with an ecstatic expression on her face. This time it is Lulu who has a motherly look, similar to that of the elderly lady at Paul's concert. Lulu observes James with pain and fear; she identifies with his struggle. The reaction of the audience is not important for her – her gaze is fixed on James; and when he is finally overtaken by the music, tears start flowing from Lulu's eyes (Figure 4). At this moment, Paul comes into the hall searching for Lulu. The concert ends with triumphant applause; Lulu goes to Paul, they embrace, and Paul says: "Look at him now, on that mountain all by himself. Nothing in the world matters, except for this moment. Did you tell him about us?" Lulu nods, but her gaze has lost its warmth, there is no love for Paul in it anymore. The camera then moves to James who is

Figure 3 James's playing is full of pain.

surrounded by admirers, but his eyes search endlessly for Lulu. In the last sequence, we see the dark stage and James playing for himself an old Flemish song that he used to play as a child. From the back, we hear Lulu saying: "I was right, wasn't I? I knew you could do it alone." Lulu and James fall into each other's arms.

One can say that Lulu's narcissism is satisfied in different ways at Paul's and James's concerts. At Paul's concert she simply identifies with the great violinist: Paul is her Ego Ideal and Lulu is concerned with the question of how she appears from the point of view of his success. When she does not get the expected narcissistic satisfaction and Paul does not acknowledge her presence, her world collapses. In the case of James, things are different: before James is successful, Lulu does not need his admiration – since James's gaze is so full of love for her and thus so overwhelming, she looks at him with contempt. This changes after his concert: when James is able

Figure 4 Lulu secretly observes James's concert.

to move his eyes from her and finish the concert, Lulu returns love, so that, at the end of the concert, her gaze expresses her love for him. This admiring gaze can easily be understood as the gaze of an artist who is delighted by the work of art she has produced: James is her masterpiece, since it is she who forced him to practice. But why does she fall in love with James, when originally she intended to help James only to regain Paul's love?

It is during their meeting in Paris that Paul, after seeing drunken James, says to Lulu: "Whenever I looked at him, I saw myself . . . I still love you, but I will always want you to be different." Lulu actually succeeds in becoming different enough, since, when Paul finds out that she has helped James, he again expresses interest in her. It is only now that Paul stops regarding her as a woman who takes from the man what is most valuable to him – his music.

When Lulu leaves Paul at the end, it can again be said that he has hurt her narcissism. Paul's remark that James is now at the top where he does not need anyone helps Lulu to recognize that Paul, who is himself at the top, still does not need her the way she wants to be needed. Although it could be said that Lulu had already felt love for James during his concert, this love, to use Hegel's term, was love *an sich* – non-recognized love. It is only Paul's remark that "opens Lulu's eyes", so that she recognizes whom she truly loves. She chooses James, because he loves her in the way she wants to be loved. Although now successful, James still needs her.

The early Lacan perceived love as the narcissistic relationship the subject establishes with the object of his or her love. By means of this narcissism, the subject primarily tries to conceal the traumatic dimension of his or her desire, which is linked to the fact that desire always remains unsatisfied, shifting from one object to another and never finding the proper one. Love thus functions as an illusory escape from desire. In *Rhapsody*, it could be said that, in her love life, Lulu masks in various ways the inconsistency of her desire: first, her lover is never the proper object of her desire (he is either too much or too little devoted to music), and second, she does not know whether she wants to be the exclusive object of the lover's desire. When Paul and Lulu have their first quarrel over his devotion to music, Lulu explains what she expects from her lover: "I want you to need me as much as I need you." Paul promises to do so, but he does not fulfill his promise, since his devotion to music is stronger than his love or need for Lulu. However, his lack of compliance with Lulu's demand makes him even more appealing to her.

Lulu's father warns her that Paul will not be able to fulfill her wish to be needed, because Paul is like himself, someone who cannot be possessed.[2] Thus it appears as if Lulu's desire is to be attracted to an unattainable object – to the man who is the double of her father. And since the father is unattainable, his double has to be so, too. But for Lacan the object of desire, the object *a*, is not simply something that is by definition unattainable, something that the subject endlessly searches for but cannot find: the object is what incites the subject's desire and is thus a cause of desire. In Lulu's case, it is thus not that she has some "free-floating" unfulfilled desire and goes from one unattainable man to another. Her desire as such is incited and put in motion only when she encounters an unattainable man. Lulu's desire for James emerges when, at his concert, James gives himself to the music and thus finally shows devotion to something other than Lulu.

Here it must again be stressed that it is always the Other's desire that keeps the subject's desire in motion. This means that, on the one hand, the woman's desire is triggered by the way she reads the man's desire (for example, the lustful way the man looks at her); but, on the other hand, the woman is intrigued by the man's desire for something other than her. So we can also say that a man becomes an object of a woman's desire when he is passionately attached to something other than her. For Lulu, it is thus not enough to see that James loves her, she wants him to be able to sacrifice her for music – only then can she desire him. But before further examining the logic of this devotion to music, let me take the example of another film, in which the musician is a woman.

THE SEVENTH VEIL, OR, SUPEREGO IN LOVE

The Seventh Veil opens with Francesca (Ann Todd) in a coma; her analyst decides to use hypnosis to uncover the "seven veils of Salome", so that her trauma can be revealed. The whole film becomes a series of flashbacks and memories that emerge during the hypnotic trance. First comes the memory of childhood, when a teenage Francesca, after the death of her parents, comes to live with her strange uncle Nicholas (James Mason), who wants to make her into a world-class pianist. Nicholas subordinates everything to fulfill this goal, and in a couple of years Francesca really succeeds. But then she falls in love with Peter and is willing to sacrifice her career for him. Nicholas ruthlessly prevents her from doing so, forcing her to travel the world; and, under his guidance, Francesca becomes a well-known artist. When the now famous Francesca returns to London, she decides to find Peter, whom she still loves, but Peter has meanwhile married. Francesca then falls in love with the painter Max, but when she intends to run away with him and abandon Nicholas, they have a car accident in which she injures her hands. When she learns about the extent of her injury, which might prevent her from continuing playing, Francesca tries to commit suicide by jumping into a river. She is rescued, but falls into a coma. At the end of the film, the psychoanalyst summons the three men (Nicholas, Peter and Max) and informs them that Francesca has been cured with the help of hypnosis and has now come to realize whom among them she truly loves. Francesca has decided that Nicholas is the one, and she and he then declare their love for one another.

In this film, the artist is a woman who becomes a great pianist after her uncle forces her to submit to a harsh drill of musical training. When Nicholas discovers that she has a great talent for music, he structures their lives entirely around her career. Nicholas is very cruel and cold in his relationship with Francesca and primarily interested in her not damaging her hands, constantly reminding her to take care of them. He becomes a superego figure for her, and it is his voice commanding her to look after her hands that, during her first concert, compels her to constantly look at them. Hearing Nicholas's voice in her head, she begins to feel that her hands are swelling, and at the end of the concert she collapses on the floor.

Comparing the concerts of the two men in *Rhapsody* with Francesca's concert in *The Seventh Veil* brings out the difference between the two films, which concerns the respective roles of gaze and voice in psychoanalysis. Gaze is related to the Ego Ideal (the subject identifies with the gaze of some person who is his or her Ideal), while voice is linked to the notion of the superego. In *Rhapsody*, the expression of Lulu's gaze at Paul's concert displays the narcissistic nature of her identification with Paul. At James's concert, Lulu's gaze is hidden: James does not know that she is observing him; he first searches for her supportive look, but when he is able to detach himself from her, her face expresses passion. In *The Seventh Veil*, Nicholas's gaze at Francesca's concert is also hidden; however, Francesca knows that Nicholas is secretly observing her, and she strongly identifies with his superego voice commanding her to look after her hands (Figures 5 and 6). Francesca does not simply take Nicholas as an Ego Ideal, she identifies with the underside of this Ideal – with the punishing superego dimension of Nicholas's authority. The relationship between Nicholas and Francesca strongly resembles the troubled rapport between a cruel father and an insecure daughter, who ostensibly tries to escape the father's overwhelming presence, but nonetheless does everything to impress him and gain his admiration. But she constantly fails in this attempt: Nicholas does not become warmer toward her; on the contrary, he imposes ever new commands.

When Francesca falls in love with the easy-going Peter, this relationship looks like a possible way to escape Nicholas's regime. Thus, it appears as if Peter remains Francesca's true object of love throughout her life and that her highest desire is to unite with him. However, here we have to distinguish between demand and desire. Francesca asks for permission to marry Peter; she is willing to sacrifice her career for him, and when she is prevented from doing so, she truly mourns his loss. But behind this demand, there is a desire related to Nicholas, since it is he who is actually

Figure 5 Nicholas observes Francesca from behind the stage.

Figure 6 Francesca on stage.

the object of her desire, although she is not conscious of this. Francesca thinks that she feels for Nicholas nothing but contempt and that her only wish is to get married and escape his terror, but Nicholas's prevention of the marriage actually allows her to recognize her true desire, which is to gain Nicholas's love.

After the car accident, Francesca thinks that she will never be able to play the piano again. Her new lover, Max, guards her at his place and keeps her from being disturbed by Nicholas; he also convinces her that he will love her whether or not she is able to play the piano. When Nicholas finally finds a way to visit Francesca, he, in contrast to Max, insists that she needs to continue playing. Max claims that he loves Francesca as herself and not as a great pianist, but Francesca wants to be loved in a different way: her decision to go with Nicholas is linked to the fact that it is Nicholas who loves Francesca in the way she wants to be loved. Nicholas loves her as a great musician and it is this type of love that inspires her desire for him. Thus, in her relationship with Nicholas, a passion for music becomes the point through which love emerges.

Before analyzing the role of music in inspiring love, let me invoke the problem of Francesca's "coma", which in psychoanalytic terms can be designated a hysterical paralysis. The symptoms of this paralysis first appear when she imagines her hands swelling and faints after the concert. After the car accident, similar symptoms emerge again, but they are not limited to her hands: this time, the whole of Francesca's body becomes lame. Francesca thus appears as a mute, almost dead body, from which life has been drained away.

In his first seminar, Lacan discusses a patient whose hands are paralyzed. This man was raised in an Islamic culture, but he insisted that he did not want to have anything to do with the Koran. Lacan was attentive precisely to this statement, since, when a patient says that he doesn't care about something, that something is usually where the trauma resides. In the course of analysis, it emerged that the patient had a traumatic childhood experience when his father was accused of being a thief. And in Islamic culture, the Koran holds that theft is to be punished by cutting off the thief's hand. For Lacan it was thus crucial to find out what the symbolic context of the patient's life was and what kind of a relationship he established in regard to this context. Although the patient consciously rejected the Koran, its symbolic structure was still unconsciously present. The subject's unconscious was thus conserving the pieces of symbolic structure, which the subject was not consciously aware of.[3] For Lacan's patient, the Koranic law was the objective structure, the big Other, that got inscribed in his symptom, although consciously he had rejected this very law.

We find a similar logic in Francesca's paralysis. Her daily life is structured around her piano practice: her uncle has devoted his whole life to making her a great pianist, and piano rehearsals are part of the rigorous ritual to which she has to submit. Francesca consciously rejects this life style: thus she desperately wants to marry and get out of the house. However, unconsciously, this structure is nonetheless at work. Her paralysis thus strongly bears the mark of the symbolic structure she wants to escape.

However, both the paralysis of Lacan's patient and Francesca's troubles with her hands need to be further examined in the light of Lacan's later teaching. The patient's symptom can easily be interpreted as an attempt to pay off the father's debt, to be punished in place of the father. But at this point we need to invoke Lacan's later theory, when he moved away from structuralism; as a result, the big Other ceased to be simply a pre-existing social symbolic structure into which the subject is born, and became a structure radically dependent on the subject. When Lacan said that the big Other doesn't exist, he stressed that it is the subject who installs the big Other in its place: the subject needs the Other in order to confirm his or her own existence.

The neurotic will do anything to keep the figure of the big Other intact. The subject might suffer endless feelings of guilt, even to the point of developing physical paralysis, merely to prevent the exposure of the lack of the Other (for example, the impotence of the father figure).

This analysis may help us perceive another aspect of Francesca's paralysis. Thus one could say that Francesca also wanted the father figure of Nicholas to remain intact; that is why she takes on the feeling of guilt. Although Nicholas should be guilty for torturing her, preventing her from living her life as she pleases, she takes the feeling of guilt upon herself and develops paralysis in order to keep his authority intact.

What role does music play for Francesca? It is obvious that she develops her passion for music via her troubled relationship with Nicholas. It is Nicholas's desire that she become a famous pianist, and at first it seems as if she merely complies with this desire when she performs music. But what actually makes her fall in love with Nicholas and what incites her desire for him is the fact that he sees in her something more than herself – a great musician.

Lacan first analyzed this object in the subject that is more than him- or herself in the context of desire, while later he links it also to drive. To understand the logic of love relations as presented in *Rhapsody* and *The Seventh Veil*, it is crucial to first explain the nature of the relationships between love and desire and between desire and drive.

LOVE AND DESIRE

What is the nature of desire in a love relationship? How is it possible for two subjects to desire each other and to form a couple? How, for example, does a loved person subjectivize him- or herself and develop desire for the loving one? When he deals with this question in the seminar on transference, Lacan introduces the myth of the two hands: one hand extends itself and tries to attract the beautiful object on the tree, while suddenly another hand emerges from the site of the object in the tree and touches the first one.[4] For Lacan, the fact that a second hand emerges in the place of the object is a miracle and not a sign of reciprocity or symmetry. The touching of the two hands does not mark the moment of unification or the formation of a pair. So what is the rapport of love?

As exemplified in Chapter 1, in the relationship between the loving and the loved, two different logics are at work. First, the loving one perceives in the other something that he or she does not have – the object *a*, which Lacan also names the *agalma*. The loving one therefore falls in love by presupposing that the loved one possesses this object, something that is in the loved one more than him- or herself. And the second logic concerns the loving subject's desire to become the object of love for the loved one.

The crucial problem for Lacan is: what makes the loving subject see the other as the object of love? His answer is: the other becomes the object of love, the desired object, precisely because he or she is a *split subject*. What is at stake in love is thus not simply that the loving subject produces the fantasy of this mythical object and transposes it onto the loved one; what makes the loved one worthy of love is that he or she is also a desiring subject. Thus, as Lacan says, the more the subject desires something, the more he or she is desired.[5]

Let us return to the problem of Socrates' refusal of love, which Chapter

1 analyzed. In Plato's *Symposium*, it is the intensity of Socrates' desire for knowledge that makes him the object of Alcibiades' desire. This intensity of Socrates' desire is what produces *agalma* – the object in him with which Alcibiades falls in love. *Agalma* thus emerges at the point where the Other is barred, where the Other is a split subject. Lacan thus says:

> Desire is at root and in its essence the desire of the Other; and it is here, properly speaking, that one finds the impetus of the birth of love, if love is what is happening in that object toward whom, led by our own desire, we are extending our hand and who, at the moment when our desire bursts into fire, for a moment offers a response in the form of that other hand that extends toward us as its desire.[6]

But the problem is that reciprocity never exists between the two subjects. Even if the loved one returns his or her hand and thus becomes a desiring subject by subjectivizing him- or herself, this does not mean that we have reached the harmony of love, since the loved one, although being now also the loving one, will also search in the other for the object, the *agalma*, that he or she does not possess.

But what makes Socrates different from these cases of loving subjects who return love? Why doesn't Socrates extend his hand toward Alcibiades and become himself a loving subject? Lacan's answer is that Socrates acts the way the analyst does when dealing with the issue of transference. The analysand also "falls in love" with the analyst because he or she takes the analyst as the *sujet supposé savoir*. But the proper response of the analyst is to insist that there is nothing in him- or herself worthy of love, that the object the other perceives in him or her is pure nothingness, emptiness. The analyst tries to retain this emptiness, he or she does not return love and does not position him- or herself as the Ideal with which the analysand should identify. Similarly, Socrates insists on this emptiness, which is why he can respond to Alcibiades' discourse by saying that it is actually the young Agathon who is the true object of Alcibiades' love.

In analysis, transference love cannot be interpreted because it is itself an interpretation, namely the "interpretation of the desire of the Other, the Other as desiring. It is a suggestive interpretation, which does not allow the Other any choice but to sustain his desire."[7] The problem of transference is that, for the analysand, transference usually emerges when he or she does not want to encounter his or her desire and instead offers him- or herself as the object of love. It is thus crucial that the analyst not comply with this demand either by returning love or by presenting him- or herself as an Ideal, as someone who should be cherished as the object of love. By refusing the demand for love, the analyst has to present him- or herself as pure emptiness, or in Lacanian terms as the object *a*, the object cause of desire. The analysand's demand for love is thus responded to by a special form of desire on the part of the analyst. So at the point where the analyst is loved, he or she returns desire as the enigmatic object *a*, since only thus will the analysand be forced to deal further with his or her own desire.

In non-analytic situations, the problem of love gets even more complicated, since we cannot say that the loved one does not return love because he or she wants to retain a presence of emptiness and thus claims that there is nothing in him or her worthy of love. This complication of love in everyday life concerns two things: first, as Chapter 1 showed, the game of courtship is always marked by the allure of the inaccessibility of the object of love, which brings love close to the logic of desire; and second, the logic of love goes beyond the logic of desire and touches on the logic of the drive. We can even say that love is placed between desire and drive as an impossible mediator between the two.

The puzzles of love in *Rhapsody* and *The Seventh Veil* clearly illuminate the problem of desire, since both films deal with the question of how the subject is desired by another, when he or she is also devoted to music. However, precisely to understand the nature of this devotion to music one needs to move from the concept of desire to the concept of drive.

FROM DESIRE TO DRIVE

Drive first needs to be understood as something left over after the subject becomes the subject of the signifier and is incorporated into a symbolic structure. When the subject becomes a speaking being, he or she is no longer able to have sex in an animal's instinctive way. However, in place of this loss, we encounter a force that essentially marks the subject by imposing constant pressure on him or her. This force is what Lacan named variously libido, drive or *lamella*. Through this naming, Lacan re-reads Freud and offers another angle on Freudian theory.

For Freud, libido primarily concerns the subject's ability to find sexual satisfaction in different ways. Aside from having sex, the subject can find this satisfaction through eating, defecating, looking, speaking, writing, etc.

Libido is always linked to a libidinal object, which is not simply a material object, but what Lacan names object *a*. We can say that, in the two films, *Rhapsody* and *The Seventh Veil*, the musician's devotion to music is such a libidinal activity in which the subject finds a special form of satisfaction.

It is crucial for the subject that only partial drives exist, and no genital drive as such. The subject is on the one hand determined by these partial drives, and on the other hand by the field of the Other, the social symbolic structure. Already for Freud, love is not to be found on the side of the drives, but on the side of the Other. And it is in this field of the Other that anything that could resemble some kind of genital drive finds its form.

The paradox of drive is therefore that it is what is left out in the process of symbolization, but this does not mean that it has no link with the field of the Other. In the scopic drive, for example, the subject is not simply someone who looks at objects: the subject makes him- or herself gazed at. A voyeur secretly observes something, but the whole point is that he wants himself to be gazed upon by the Other. In the scopic drive the subject makes himself the object that complements the Other, who is supposed to enjoy gazing at him. The subject thus needs the big Other, its imagined virtual gaze, in order to set in motion the drive and to obtain satisfaction. Lacan mentions here the flasher: his victim's horror or uncomfortable reaction to his exposure bring satisfaction to the flasher as long as he knows that he has been gazed upon in his act, i.e. that this act was registered by the virtual gaze of the big Other. The same goes for the sadist: the pain he imposes on the victim has to be looked upon by the Other.

How, then, are we to understand Lacan's thesis that "the course of the drive is the only form of transgression that is permitted to the subject in relation to the pleasure principle"?[8] The pleasure principle is to be understood here as the symbolic law, the safeguard of the homeostasis, which tries to prevent the irruption of *jouissance* that is linked to the satisfaction of drive. Already for Freud drive is what lies beyond the pleasure principle, but Lacan adds to this the notion that the transgression linked to drive is in some way permitted by the symbolic law itself: insofar as drive always involves the Other, the subject gets from the Other a kind of permission for his or her transgression.

Drive and desire each have a different relation to the symbolic structure. Desire is essentially linked to law, since it always searches for something that is prohibited or unavailable. The logic of desire is: "It is prohibited to do this, but I will nonetheless do it." Drive, in contrast, does not care about prohibition: it is not concerned about overcoming the law. Drive's logic is: "I do not want to do this, but I am nonetheless doing it." Thus, we have an opposite logic in drive, when the subject does not desire to do something, but nonetheless enjoys doing exactly that. As, for example, James in *Rhapsody* gives up on music since he desires simply to be with Lulu, but his devotion is like a death drive, which does not give him peace – not playing music brings him to perdition: he becomes a lost alcoholic. Similarly, Francesca in *The Seventh Veil* does not want to play and desires just to get married and to escape Nicholas's torture, but then the fear that she might actually not be able to play after the accident brings her to the verge of suicide. Stopping playing means death for her.

Drive paradoxically always finds satisfaction, while desire has to remain unsatisfied, endlessly going from one object to another, positing new limits and prohibitions. Drive is thus a constant pressure, a circulation around the object *a*, which produces *jouissance* – a painful satisfaction. The object *a*, the object around which drive circulates, thus needs to be understood as a special kind of satisfaction: "The object that corresponds to drive is *satisfaction as object*."[9] In this search for satisfaction, drive resembles perversion.

For perverts, it is essential that they search for sexual satisfaction outside simple copulation. Perverts differ from neurotics who always lack satisfaction and thus go from one object to another, not knowing what they want, endlessly questioning the nature of their desire. Perverts, in contrast, are satisfied: they find the object and thus also sexual satisfaction. That is why perverts rarely demand analysis, or they demand it only when they are perplexed as to whether or not the satisfaction that they have found is the proper one.[10] In the same way as perverts do not find sexual satisfaction in taking another person as a whole, but are usually turned on by some particular object (a fetish), drive also is not directed toward another subject: there is only drive toward the libidinal object, toward "a partial satisfaction as the object".[11] Drive thus circulates around the partial object, the object *a*, and this circulation precisely constitutes the satisfaction. If desire constantly questions, drive presents an inertia where questioning stops. Here the dynamic of drive resembles perversion because the pervert also does not ask for permission.

In the final instance, drive is always the death drive, the destructive force that endlessly undermines the points of support that the subject has found in the symbolic universe. In regard to drive, desire plays a paradoxical role of protection, since desire, by being subordinated to the law, pacifies the lawless drive and the horrible *jouissance* that is linked to it. The subject of desire is the subject of identification: this is the subject who constantly searches for points of support in the symbolic universe, the ideals with which he or she can identify and thus achieve an identity. Such a point of identification can be a teacher, lover, analyst, etc. But on the level of drive, there is no identification anymore, there is only *jouissance*.

Desire is sustained by a fantasy scenario that masks the *jouissance* of the drive; it is therefore trapped inside the pleasure principle, while drive goes beyond this principle. Paradoxically, the subject is always happy at the level of drive: although he or she can actually suffer terribly and tries to get rid of the enormous pressure imposed by drive, this suffering brings about a painful satisfaction.[12]

The major issue in Lacan's late work is how, in the course of the analytic treatment, the subject can move from being endlessly perturbed by the desire of the Other to dealing with his or her drive. In order to clarify this point, let us return briefly to *Rhapsody*, in which James and Lulu, in a touching way, connect one with another even before they become a couple, when James plays an old Flemish song and Lulu remembers that she also knows this song. This melody reminds both of them of a scene from childhood. For Lulu, this was the song her nanny used to play. And for James, this was the first song he learned to play on the piano, but it reminds him of a teacher that used to constantly beat him on his fingers. James always fantasized that when he became a successful pianist he would invite this professor to his concert and seat him in the back row. But the fact that the teacher died four years before was for James the last stroke on his fingers.

Such a scenario of how to punish the teacher stages a typical fantasy of the neurotic who enjoys plotting how he or she will punish the person who had in the past supposedly stolen his or her *jouissance*. This person is usually a parent or a parental figure, and the neurotic will be able to organize his or her whole life around the fantasy of how to get even with this person. Analysis should bring the neurotic to the point where he or she no longer has the need to punish the Other and ceases doing things to get even with the Other or to please the Other. The subject, therefore, stops searching for the impossible answer to the question what kind of an object he or she is in the desire of the Other, which also means that the subject has no need to punish the Other anymore.

A radical change happens for James when he finishes the concert without counting on provoking the Other, for example, by punishing the teacher or impressing Lulu. It is only when he stopped blaming the Other (his professor) for stealing his *jouissance* that he could let his own drive for music follow its path. James's playing at the end of the film thus seems completely different: in the melody of the old Flemish song there is no longer any pain of revenge.

Although, in contrast to the intersubjectivity of desire, drive is in a way essentially solipsistic, "something the subject can't help or stop in him- or herself",[13] it is paradoxically also what attracts us to the other, what makes another person the object of our love. However, here we have to invoke again the partial character of drive. When we take a whole person as our libidinal object we are not at the level of drive but at the level of love: we always love the other as a whole. When deeply in love, we are by definition not aware of what attracts us to some person, everything about him or her looks fascinating, even odd habits at first seem to be endearing. This is because in love our fascination makes the other person complete, Ideal. Our perception of love, therefore, masks the fact that we actually became attracted to the object *a*, to what the other actually does not possess.

So how does the object *a* relate to the distinction between drive and desire? On the one hand, the loving subject is attracted to the other because the other is also a desiring subject, which means both that the loved subject is perturbed by the question: what does the other desire? – and also that the loving subject hopes to become the object of the other's desire. So we can agree with Lacan's thesis from the seminar on transference that we love the other because he or she is a split, desiring subject. But, on the other hand, what makes the other the object of love is actually the very *jouissance* that is linked to the way the other satisfies his or her drive: the loving subject is perturbed by and attracted to the *jouissance* of the other. In racist hatred (let us remember that hatred is always the counterpart of love), the subject primarily objects to the other because of the way he or she enjoys ("their" music, "their" food, etc.); this ungraspable *jouissance* of the other then generates the fantasies about the others. In love, we encounter the same attraction (which can easily turn into repulsion) to the *jouissance* of the other: this *jouissance* is discernible in the gaze of the other, in his or her voice, smell, smile, laughter . . .

In the melodramas that I have analyzed, the subjects' devotion to music has to be understood as a libidinal activity, which is essentially linked to drive. That is why it can be said that love triangles, as the one in *Rhapsody*, have a mark of perversion, since the musician gets more sexual satisfaction from playing the musical instrument than from being with a woman and, paradoxically, the woman finds the musician more attractive because of his devotion to music.

In his seminar on anxiety, Lacan mysteriously claims that it is only love that allows *jouissance* to condescend to desire.[14] If desire has to be understood as always being tied to the Other in the sense that "desire is desire of the Other", one has to add to this point that what is behind the Other's desire, what in the final instance keeps our desire in motion, is the unbearable *jouissance* of the Other. What attracts us in the Other is thus not simply his or her desire but drive – which forces the Other into some activity, regardless of how painful this activity could be for him or her. And artists are so attractive as the objects of love because the drive that masters them in their inner selves is able to incite their artistic genius.

OF MALE AND FEMALE GENIUSES

How does sexual difference inscribe itself into the triangle of love, desire and drive? Both *Rhapsody* and *The Seventh Veil* stage a patriarchal scenario of the way an artistic genius ties up with love. In *Rhapsody*, the woman has no interest in her own career, but only in the career of her lover: the man is marked by drive, and woman becomes just a vehicle for his success, but the vehicle that he must be able to abandon in order to truly gain the woman's love. *The Seventh Veil* displays a different structure: the woman discovers music only through the paternal figure who forces her to practice; later she becomes essentially marked by music (remember, the trauma of her paralysis of hands) – but the real reconciliation occurs when, at the end, she marries her mentor. Here, the woman is able to develop her artistic genius only via her strong identification with a father figure: the separation from him would have brought to an end also her musical practice.

The Red Shoes, which also focuses on the dilemma between love and profession, stages the inverted version of the same patriarchal scenario. After the success of the ballet "The Red Shoes", based on Andersen's fairy tale, a ballerina, Victoria Page (Moira Shearer), under the guidance of a severe ballet impresario Boris Lermontov (Anton Wallbrook), becomes an international star. But, in contrast to *The Seventh Veil*, the woman's desire for art is not primarily the result of her identification with her mentor. Victoria herself has a strong devotion to dance. When Victoria first encounters Lermontov, he cynically asks her: "Why do you want to dance?" Victoria responds: "Why do you want to live?" "Because I must", says Lermontov, and Victoria replies: "This is my answer, too." Dance is for Victoria something she simply has to do. And this does not change when she falls in love with a young conductor, Julian. However, Lermontov's perception is that one cannot have it both ways – to dance and to be in love. Lermontov thus dismisses Julian from the company and demands that Victoria sacrifice her love for Julian, but she does not comply with this demand and quits the company too. After some time, Lermontov wants again to stage "The Red Shoes" and invites Victoria to return to the company. Victoria agrees, but before the premiere, Julian confronts her with the question: whom does she like more, him or dance? She does not answer, but desperately looks at her red ballet shoes. For Julian this is a proof that she prefers dance, and he stormily leaves her dressing-room. Lermontov tries to convince Victoria that now she can completely devote herself to dance, but at the moment when she is expected to go on stage, she runs out of the building and jumps under a train. With her last strength she asks Julian to take off her red shoes. Victoria had thus followed the destiny of the heroine from Andersen's fairy tale who also could not put off her red shoes which brought her to death.

In *The Red Shoes*, we have a father figure in the persona of the impresario Lermontov, but here it is not the case that the woman is secretly in love with him. On the contrary, one can speculate that Lermontov himself feels more than a professional attachment toward Victoria, although he feigns indifference. Furthermore, a crucial difference from *The Seventh Veil* is that Victoria dances for her own enjoyment, because she "must" and not because she is forced to by her mentor. Although her career progresses greatly under Lermontov's severe rule, her passion for dance is not itself dependent on her identification with the father figure. Victoria is nonetheless perturbed by the dilemma of love and profession and, when she is forced to make a choice between the two, she commits suicide. Her ballet shoes become her object of drive whose pressure she cannot get rid of: they take a grip on her and finally bring her to death.

In contrast to *Rhapsody*, in *The Red Shoes* we do not have an artist who must first totally devote himself to art and show that he is able to survive without the woman in order to become a worthy object of her love. If Victoria were to choose dance, she would have lost her husband, and the only solution to this impossible choice between love and dance is death. In the patriarchal structure as presented in *Rhapsody*, a man can have both, love and profession, if, first, he is able to devote himself totally to profession (i.e. forget the woman), and, second, if the woman is not devoted to any profession of her own. In this case, the man is under the pressure of drive which forces him to play music, and when he gets social recognition for his art, he becomes the object of woman's desire. In *The Red Shoes* this scenario is not feasible, since a man has his career too, and one can speculate that the fact that he is a successful composer contributes to Victoria's falling in love with him. Victoria and Julian had a happy love relation while Victoria put her career on hold so that Julian could focus on his. When Victoria decides to dance again in "The Red Shoes", Julian does not support her decision. At the opening night of "The Red Shoes" Julian is supposed to conduct a concert at Covent Garden, but instead he comes to Victoria and demands that she choose between ballet and him. With this demand, Julian is primarily asking Victoria to abandon Lermontov. Although Victoria is not emotionally interested in Lermontov, he is none-theless a person who sees in her her artistic genius. The situation is similar to that in *The Seventh Veil*, where the woman strongly identifies with the fact that her mentor sees in her something more than herself – a drive, which is sublimated in her artistic profession. Lermontov appears an asexual character, for whom there is no life outside ballet. He resembles Nicholas who also lives a lonely life and is totally devoted to music. While the difference between Francesca and Victoria is that the latter is very much devoted to her art even before she meets her mentor, they both identify with what their mentor sees in them.

If a woman falls in love with her mentor, as in *The Seventh Veil*, we have a happy ending; if not, the woman commits suicide. The triangle of love, desire and drive forms a harmonious union, when a man (mentor) is attracted by the artistic genius in the woman artist (by her drive): she then acquires fame and becomes a socially recognized artist via her identification with him. This identification first looks like hate or indifference, but then she actually develops desire for her mentor and falls in love with him. While in the case of a man's being the artist, as in *Rhapsody*, the structure is different: with the help of a woman, who is some kind of a surrogate mentor (his teacher is the actual mentor), a man brings his career to its peak and when he demonstrates that he can survive without her, she truly falls in love with him.

It appears that drive in a woman is something seductive and horrifying at the same time, and has to be subordinated to the constraints of some symbolic relationship with her mentor if she is truly to become a successful artist. A woman who is not subordinated in such a way becomes the fearful figure of a man-eater. In the next chapter, I will analyze the Sirens, those mythical men-eaters, as beings of drive. Was not Jacqueline du Pré a real-life example of such a man-eater? She subordinated everything to her art of cello-playing and used men just as a side excitement: she had numerous lovers, among them her sister's husband; she picked men up and dropped them as she pleased. When she was diagnosed with multiple sclerosis, her illness appeared to her family almost like God's punishment for her excessive life style. The excessiveness did not concern simply her turbulent love life, but the fact that she completely subordinated men to her devotion to music: since no man was able to constrain her artistic genius, the illness did the task. Her body became more and more paralyzed, which finally prevented her from playing.

From the cases I have analyzed, one can conclude that for a woman it is not enough that her drive gets sublimated and thus incites the work of art; she also needs to be "pacified" via her attachment to a mentor or another man in order to allow her artistic genius to flourish. While a man has to show that his attachment to music comes first, a woman has to show that her devotion to art comes second, after her attachment to a mentor.

But it is not only that excessive female *jouissance* has to be restrained in order to allow a woman to become an artist; excessive female *jouissance* can endanger also a male artist. In *Humoresque*, Helen (Joan Crawford), a middle-aged married woman, falls in love with a young violinist Paul (John Garfield) and helps him with his career. Helen is portrayed as a woman who drinks too much, is admired by men and is excessively devoted to Paul. Paul's mother is opposed to Helen: she perceives her as a woman who will endanger her son's career. The mother has also already found a girl who would be an ideal wife for her son, since she would subordinate her life completely to his career. Although Paul loves Helen, he does not show very much enthusiasm for marrying her after learning that she has divorced her husband. For Paul music comes first, and the film ends with Paul making a triumphant concert, while Helen commits suicide.

Mary Ann Doane's excellent analysis of this film stresses the danger of

Helen's excessive desire for Paul's career.[15] But, in regard to the above-mentioned Lacanian distinction between desire and drive, my point is that what is excessive in Helen is her *jouissance*, which is linked to drive and not desire. It is not that Helen simply desires Paul, she painfully enjoys her attachment to him which at the end brings her to death. This *jouissance* has to be somehow pacified by the symbolic order (via a marriage contract, for example); otherwise it is perceived as a deadly threat either for men or for the woman herself. In this excessive *jouissance*, Helen resembles the Sirens from Greek mythology: like them, she commits suicide by walking into the sea.

Let us recall that Helen acted as Paul's mentor: when a woman provides the conditions for man's success, he has to *detach himself from her* at some point – if he does not do so, she has to annihilate herself. In the case of the man's being a woman's mentor, the situation is turned around: the woman has to *retain her attachment to him* – if she does not do so, she either abandons her career or commits suicide. So why are women much more prone to suicidal self-annihilation? And why do men feel threatened by the excessive woman's attachment to them? The answer can only be provided by a further examination of the nature of feminine *jouissance*, which is the topic of the next chapter.

NOTES

1. When Lulu is Paul's girlfriend, his professor reminds her of the impossibility of competing with music: "A great violinist might only be a fair husband. And a great husband can only be a fair violinist." "Couldn't he be both?" objects Lulu. "He might, but it is bigamy if he loves music as much as his wife. Unless, she loves music, too. Do you?" Lulu responds: "No, but I want to learn it." She insists that she would love Paul even if he was not a great violinist, and the professor questions whether Paul would be able to live with this reality.
2. Lulu's relationship with her father in a peculiar way influences her choice of a lover. At the beginning he does not like Paul and Lulu's choice of him appears at first as a way of rebelling against her father. However, behind this is Lulu's desire to seduce her father. Later the father perversely plays the role of intermediary, when he organizes their reunion in Paris. The father thus regards Paul on the one hand as his competitor, and on the other hand as his double.

3. See Jacques Lacan, *Seminar I: Freud's Papers on Technique (1953–1954)*, trans. John Forrester and Sylvia Tomaselli, New York: Norton 1988, pp. 196, 197. See also, Colette Soler, "The Symbolic Order", in *Reading Seminars I and II: Return to Freud*, ed. Bruce Fink, Richard Feldstein and Maire Jaanus, Albany: State University of New York Press 1995.
4. See Jacques Lacan, *Le Séminaire, livre VIII: Le transfert*, Paris: Editions du Seuil 1991, p. 67. See also Jacques-Alain Miller, "Les deux métaphores de l'amour", *La Cause Freudienne* 18 (1995), p. 219.
5. Lacan, *Le Séminaire, livre VIII: Le transfert*, p. 156.
6. Ibid., p. 212.
7. Michel Silvestre, *Demain la psychanalyse*, Paris: Navarin 1987, p. 60.
8. Jacques Lacan, *The Four Fundamental Concepts of Psycho-Analysis*, trans. Alan Sheridan, New York: Norton 1977, p. 183.
9. Jacques-Alain Miller, "On Perversion", in *Reading Seminars I and II: Return to Freud*, p. 313.
10. See Bruce Fink, *A Clinical Introduction to Lacanian Psychoanalysis: Theory and Technique*, Cambridge, MA: Harvard University Press 1997.
11. Miller, "On Perversion".
12. Jacques-Alain Miller, *Donc*, unpublished seminar (1993–94), 18 May 1994.
13. Lacan, *The Four Fundamental Concepts of Psycho-Analysis*, p. 53.
14. Jacques Lacan, *Angoisse*, unpublished seminar (1962–63), 13 March 1963.
15. Mary Ann Doane, *Desire to Desire*, Bloomington: Indiana University Press, 1987.

3

THE SILENCE OF
FEMININE *JOUISSANCE*

When we hear the sound of a siren, we immediately think, "Danger!" or maybe even, "Death!" During wartime, the codified signal of sirens warns of enemy attacks; and during peacetime, sirens alert people to fires or medical emergencies. In some countries, sirens are also used on national holidays to invoke solemn events from the past. In the former Yugoslavia, sirens went off every year at 3 p.m. on the day commemorating Tito's death; and in Israel, sirens announce the moment of silence on Memorial Day, when people remember the soldiers who fell during the war for independence. When sirens sound, life is interrupted: people stop, the traffic stops, and for a minute everyone stands motionless. The sound of sirens invokes the stillness of time: it freezes the moment and petrifies the hearers.

In their paralyzing effect, today's public sirens very much resemble their predecessors, the ancient Sirens of classical mythology – half-human beings, half-birds, who lived on an island to which they enticed sailors with their seductive singing.[1] Those sailors who succumbed to the Sirens' song immediately died. As a result, the island was covered with piles of white bones, the remains of the perished sailors. Hence, the very setting in which the Sirens dwelled was filled with death. Whenever a ship approached the Sirens' island, the wind died away, the sea became still, and the waves flattened into a calm sheet of glass: the sailors entered the land where life is fixed forever. The Sirens themselves were neither dead nor alive: they were creatures in between – the living dead. Or, as Jean-Pierre Vernant says, they were, on the one hand, pure desire, and, on the other hand, pure death: they were "death in its most brutally monstrous aspect: no funeral, no tomb, only the corpse's decomposition in the open air".[2]

As many theorists of Greek mythology have observed, the Sirens present a danger to particular men's lives, while they also challenge the social order as such, especially the family structure. In the *Odyssey* we thus read:

"Whoever draws too close, off guard, and catches the Sirens' voices in the air – no sailing home for him, no wife rising to meet him, no happy children beaming up at their father's face."[3] The danger the Sirens pose to family life and, more generally, to the social order is supposedly linked to their status as creatures that are closer to nature than to culture.[4] In the context of psychoanalytic theory, the trouble their bestiality presents for culture as well as for individual men has to be placed in the context of the subject's confrontation with that special form of "cultured" animality which is known as drive. But before we put the Sirens under the lens of psychoanalytic theory, let us first recount some aspects of Odysseus' encounter with them.

Curiously, we learn more about the deadliness of the Sirens from Circe's warnings to Odysseus than from Odysseus' own account of his adventure with them. Odysseus sees no heap of bones around the Sirens' island. He only says that the Sirens encouraged him to drop anchor and listen to their honey-sweet voices, which bring pleasure and wisdom to man. The Sirens thus boasted to Odysseus: "We know all the pains Achaeans and Trojans once endured on the spreading plain of Troy when the gods willed it so – all that comes to pass on the fertile earth, we know it all!"[5]

These words incite Odysseus' desire to stop and surrender himself to the Sirens' lure: he is willing to endure a collusion with the singers that excludes everything else.[6] But the mystery of the *Odyssey* is that we never learn what the Sirens actually sing about. Did the Sirens ever sing, and if they did sing, why doesn't Homer recount this song? Pietro Pucci gives two explanations for this. First, "the *Odyssey* presents the Sirens as the embodiment of the paralyzing effects of the Iliadic poetics because their song binds its listeners obsessively to the fascination of death."[7] Death is therefore something that lies at the center of the *Odyssey*, the song of survival, but it is also something that must be left unspoken. The second explanation concerns the fact that "the *Odyssey*'s own sublime poetry cannot be inferior to that of the Sirens. No text can incorporate the titillating promise of a song as sublime as the Sirens' without implying that this sublimity resides in the incorporating text itself."[8] Thus, the *Odyssey* itself has to be understood as the embodiment of the Sirens' song. Their song is "the negative, absent song that enables its replacement – the *Odyssey* – to become what it is".[9] In sum, the Sirens' song is left unsung either because death as such is something that has to be left unspoken, or because the *Odyssey* itself comes to incorporate or represent their song. In both cases, it stands as an empty, unutterable point in the *Odyssey*, which, with the allusion to deadly pleasure, brings a sublime quality to the poem.

Tzvetan Todorov gives another answer to the question why we know nothing about the Sirens' song. His thesis is that the Sirens said just one thing to Odysseus: we are singing. In other words, the Sirens' song is a self-referential claim that there is a song. And death is always linked to this song. It is not only that the listeners die upon hearing the Sirens' song; if the Sirens fail to seduce their prey, they themselves commit suicide. (Some post-Homeric interpretations of the *Odyssey* maintain that the Sirens threw themselves from the rock into the sea when Odysseus escaped their lure.) Thus, the only way for the Sirens to escape death is to seduce and then kill those who hear them. On another level, this also explains why we do not know the secret of the Sirens' song:

> The song of the Sirens is, at the same time, that poetry which must disappear for there to be life, and that reality which must die for literature to be born. The song of the Sirens must cease for a song about the Sirens to appear . . . By depriving the Sirens of life, Odysseus has given them, through the intermediary of Homer, immortality.[10]

In other words, the Sirens' song is the point in the narrative that has to remain unspoken for the narrative to gain consistency. It is a point of self-referentiality that a story has to omit in order to attain the status of a story. From the Lacanian perspective, this empty point is another name for the real, the unsymbolizable kernel around which the symbolic forms itself. This kernel is not simply something prior to symbolization; it is also what remains: what is left over from, or, better, the failure of symbolization. The Sirens' song is the real that has to be left out for the story of the *Odyssey* to achieve form. However, there is no song of the Sirens before the story of the *Odyssey*. The Sirens' song is thus, on the one hand, that which incites the *Odyssey* as narration, while, on the other hand, it is also that which results from this narration: its remainder, which cannot be recounted.

What kind of knowledge of the past do the Sirens have? In regard to this knowledge, there is a significant difference between the Sirens and the Muses, who are also supposed to have voices that are delicately clear, immortal, tirelessly sweet and unbroken. The Muses are the daughters of Zeus and the Titaness Mnemosyne (Memory); as the fruits of their parents' nine nights of lovemaking, the Muses became the singers who preside over thought and artistic creativity.[11] The Muses bring memory to their listeners, along with the divine help that produces inspiration: "according to Hesiod, a singer (in other words a servant of the Muses) has only to celebrate the deeds of men of former days or to sing of the gods, and any man beset by troubles will forget them instantly."[12] The memory of the past that the Muses bring is thus essentially linked to forgetfulness.

With the Sirens, the knowledge of the past has a different meaning: "The Sirens know the secrets of the past, but it is a past that has no future life in the 'remembering' of successive generations."[13] How is one to understand here the difference between knowledge and memory? For Lacan, memory primarily has to do with the non-remembering of trauma, the real on which the subject centers his or her very being. When we tell our stories, it is at the point where we touch the real that our words fail, but fail so as to always come back to the trauma without being able to articulate it:

> The subject in himself, the recalling of his biography, all this goes only to a certain limit, which is known as the real ... An adequate thought, *qua* thought, at the level at which we are, always avoids – if only to find itself again later in everything – the same thing. Here the real is that which always comes back to the same place – to the place where the subject in so far as he thinks, where the *res cogitans*, does not meet it.[14]

The subject forms memory in order to achieve consistency, to fashion a story that would enable him to escape the traumatic real.

In regard to the difference between the Muses and the Sirens, we can say that only the Muses provide memory, since they enable their listeners to forget the traumas of their life, while the Sirens put the listeners in touch with what Lacan calls the *knowledge in the real*, that knowledge which the listeners do not want to know anything about. Inspired by the memory that the Muses provide, their listeners are able to create works of art, while those who hear the knowledge offered by the Sirens' song immediately die. In a different theoretical context, Adorno and Horkheimer make the same point when they claim that the Sirens' singing cannot be perceived as art precisely because of the way it deals with the past:

> [the Sirens'] allurement is that of losing oneself in the past ... The compulsion to rescue what is gone as what is living instead of using it as the material of progress was appeased only in art, to which history itself appertains as a presentation of past life. So long as past declines to pass as cognition and is thus separated from practice, social practice tolerates it as it tolerates pleasure. But the Sirens' song has not yet been rendered powerless by reduction to the condition of art.[15]

The past in the Sirens' song has not yet been symbolized, it has not become a memory; such an unsymbolized past is traumatic for the listener, since it evokes something primordial, something between nature and culture that the subject does not want to remember. And for Odysseus, it becomes essential to symbolize his encounter with the Sirens and to form a narrative about them. Here Odysseus significantly differs from his colleagues, whose ears were closed with wax to avoid succumbing to the voices of the Sirens. Odysseus wants to hear their singing. Circe, who instructed him how to escape the Sirens' enchantment, also gave him a mandate to remember this event and recount it to his colleagues and to Penelope. He is thus obliged to form a memory of his encounter with the Sirens, i.e. to cover up the trauma that they present.

As explained in the previous chapter, the Lacanian term for this "knowledge in the real" which resists symbolization is *drive*, the self-sufficient closed circuit of the deadly compulsion-to-repeat. The paradox is this: that which cannot ever be memorized, symbolized by way of its inclusion into the narrative frame, is not some fleeting moment of the past, forever lost, but the very insistence of drive as that which *cannot ever be forgotten* in the first place, since it repeats itself incessantly.

The problem for the subject is that he or she is nothing except through the love and desire of others. The subject by him- or herself has no value. Recognizing this fact causes the subject's devastating depressive moods. So, it turns out that the subject is not the phallus that would complement the Other. The Other can function very well without the subject. And to overcome this traumatic truth, the subject endlessly tries to leave a mark on the Other, on the social symbolic structure, on history, etc. However, the subject can find a special form of happiness when he or she is not at all concerned with the Other, i.e. through *jouissance* which pertains to drive.

One can discern this *jouissance* in the partial drives related to the voice and gaze. It is in the tonality of the voice, for example, that we encounter *jouissance* – this is where the surplus enjoyment comes into being as something that eludes signification. This excessive *jouissance* in voice is what makes the voice both fascinating and deadly.[16] If we take as an example the diva, it is clear that the very enjoyment of opera resides in her voice. At its peak, her voice assumes the status of the object detached from the body. The singer has to approach "self-annihilation as a subject in order to offer himself or herself as pure voice. The success of this process is the condition for the dissolution of the incongruity between singer and role, a dissolution that . . . is at the foundation of the lyric arts."[17] But if this process does not succeed, the public sometimes reacts with violence. The singer who fails to produce this effect of the object detached from the subject reopens the incongruity between object and subject and thus becomes "a failing subject": "the singer is cast back by the public into the position of object, but now a fallen object, a piece of refuse, to be greeted in kind with rotten egg or ripe tomato – or . . . with the vocal stand-in for refuse: booing and catcalls."[18] The public reacts so violently because it is denied its moment of ecstasy; its fantasy of finally possessing the inaccessible object has fallen through. And the same goes for the Sirens: if they do not succeed in seduction, they are punished. Many stories about the Sirens stress their failure to seduce with their voices. Unsuccessful singing contests with the Muses supposedly caused the Sirens to lose their wings. Later they tried to outcharm Orpheus' lyre, but failed again and as a result supposedly committed suicide.

THE OTHER'S DESIRE, THE OTHER'S *JOUISSANCE*

For psychoanalysis, the problem of the encounter between Odysseus and the Sirens thus concerns the logic of desire and drive: how does the subject react to the drive in the Other? How does the subject respond to hearing the seductive voice of the Other? Could it be that the desire that the subject (Odysseus, in our case) develops in response to the luring Other (the Sirens) is actually a shield against the destructive nature of the drive? In this precise sense, one is tempted to claim that the Lacanian object *a*, the object-cause of desire, is none other than drive itself: that which arouses the subject's desire for another subject is the very specific mode of the Other's *jouissance* embodied in the object *a*. As pointed out in Chapter 2, this *jouissance* of the Other (which provokes either love or hate) gets inscribed in the gaze of the Other, his or her voice, smell, smile, laughter, etc., i.e. all the features which exert an irresistible attraction on another subject.

In Homer there is a certain ignorance at work in the Sirens' lure: they would like to trap Odysseus, but they are not at all struck by him, i.e. he is not the object of their desire. In Chapters 1 and 2, I dealt with cases of love in which the heroes question the desire of the Other. Why is the desire of the Other such a problem for the subject? For Lacan, this dilemma concerns the subject's very being; the first formulation of this question is what was the subject's place in his or her parents' desire? The subject tries to answer this question by way of forming a fundamental fantasy, a story of his or her origins that will provide the grounds for his or her very being.

The desire of the Other incites horror on the side of the subject, i.e. it produces anxiety. This anxiety arises because the Other's desire remains an enigma to the subject; which also means that the subject can never really know what kind of an object he or she is for the Other. Lacan exemplifies this anxiety by asking us to imagine one day encountering a giant female praying mantis; as it happens, we are wearing a mask, but we do not know what kind of a mask it is: we do not know if it is a male or female mask. If it is a male mask, we can, of course, expect to be devoured by the female praying mantis. This example returns us to the subject's encounter with deadly feminine creatures, such us Medusa or the Sirens. In this encounter, the subject's urgent question is: what kind of mask am I wearing? In other words, what kind of an object am I for her? Am I a man or a woman? This is the male hysteric's question. He has doubts about his sex and his being and therefore expects to get an answer from the Other, just as a female hysteric does. And, to obtain this answer, he posits himself as the ultimate object of the Other's desire, but the object whose allure is linked to the fact that he always vanishes and can never be possessed.

Because most men are not hysterics but obsessionals, the question is: what is the obsessional strategy toward the monstrous female? In contrast to the hysteric, who sustains her desire as unsatisfied, the obsessional maintains his desire as impossible. While for the hysteric every object of desire is unsatisfactory, for the obsessional this object appears too satisfactory, that is why the encounter with this object has to be prevented by all means. The hysteric, by constantly eluding the Other, slipping away as object, maintains the lack in the Other. She wants to be the ultimate object of the desire of the Other; but she nonetheless prevents this from happening, and by doing so keeps her desire unsatisfied. But the obsessional maintains his desire as impossible and does so in order to negate the Other's desire.[19]

The obsessional wants to be in charge of the situation; he plans his activities in detail. An encounter with the woman who is the object of his desire will be thought out well in advance; everything will be programmed and organized, all to prevent something unexpected from happening. The unexpected here concerns desire and *jouissance*. The obsessional tries to master his desire and desire of the Other by never giving up thinking or talking. His strategy is to plug up his lack with signifiers and thus to avoid the object of his desire. Lacan also points out that the obsessional does not want to vanish or to fade as a subject, which happens when the subject is eclipsed by the object of his desire and *jouissance*. The obsessional tries to demonstrate that he is the master of his own desire and that no object is capable of making him vanish.[20] Even during sexual intercourse, he will go on planning, thinking and talking, always in efforts to control his *jouissance* and the *jouissance* of the Other.

This obsessional strategy can best be exemplified by the case of a man who waited for two nights for a telephone call from the woman who was the object of his love. In the middle of the night he got the idea that the phone might not be working, and repeatedly picked up the receiver to check the dial tone. The man knew, of course, that picking up the receiver would hinder the woman's efforts to call him, so as soon as he was convinced that the phone was working, he quickly put the receiver down. But after a short while, he would repeat the test procedure. He continued this ritual throughout the night to the point of utter exhaustion. And after two nights, he fell into a serious crisis, which brought him to analysis.[21]

Odysseus' position is obsessional: he resorts to a series of strategies to keep the *jouissance* of the Other and his own desire for the Other at bay. Odysseus thus performs a whole ritual to prevent a genuine encounter with the Sirens. It can even be said that he finds his *jouissance* precisely in this ritual of thinking and planning his escape from the Sirens' lure.

While the hysteric endlessly questions the desire of the Other, the obsessional does not want to know anything about this desire. Thus he wants to escape from situations that might involve confrontation, or might in any way disturb his equilibrium. Thus the encounter with the desiring Other becomes the most horrible thing for the obsessional. While the hysteric deals with the dilemma, "Am I a man or a woman?", the obsessional agonizes over the question, "Am I dead or alive?" He hopes that with the death of the desiring Other, who continually imposes obligations on him, he will finally be free to live. The obsessional is thus a special kind of living dead, since the rituals and prohibitions he imposes on himself make him a robot-like creature, apparently drained of desire.

Odysseus also acts in an obsessional way in his passion to narrate his encounter with the Sirens. It is well known that obsessionals find great joy not only in planning the encounter with the object of their desire and at the same time preventing this from happening, but also in narrating this failure, in creating a story about it. Odysseus also has been mandated to recount his meeting with the Sirens, and his *jouissance* is at work not only in planning how to avoid an actual encounter with them, but also in telling others about this missed encounter.

In sum: for both the hysteric and the obsessional, it is crucial to understand their problems with desire as defences against *jouissance*. The hysteric, for example, wants to be the ever-elusive object of the Other's desire, but she does not want to be the object of the Other's *jouissance*. She does not simply want to be a partial object through which the Other enjoys, but something else – the unattainable object of desire. The hysteric masquerades herself as a phallic woman with the intention of covering the lack in the Other, to make the Other complete. Since this attempt always fails, she needs to repeat her seductive strategy again and again. Through seduction, the hysteric tries to provoke the Other's desire for her, which will, of course, never be satisfied. Although the hysteric may enjoy this game of seduction and non-satisfaction, she cannot deal with the situation when the Other takes her as his object of *jouissance* and not simply as the inaccessible object of desire. The hysteric is therefore attracted to the desire of the Other, but horrified by his *jouissance*.

Let us exemplify this aversion to the Other's *jouissance* with the help of a short story by O. Henry, "The Memento". This story is about a young Broadway dancer, Lynnete, who decides to change her life: she gives up dancing, moves to a small village and falls happily in love with the local pastor, from whom she conceals her dishonorable past. Rumor has it that the pastor was unhappily in love sometime before and that he keeps a secret memento of his beloved locked in a box. One day, Lynnete finds and opens this box. What she discovers presents an absolute horror for her: in the box is one of the very garters that she, as a Broadway dancer, used to throw into the audience at the end of each performance. After this discovery, Lynnete flees from the village and, disillusioned, returns to the Broadway theater.

The story makes it clear that the pastor did not know that he had fallen in love with the same woman twice. When Lynnete questions him about his past love, the pastor simply explains that some time ago he was infatuated by a woman whom he did not really know. He admired this woman only from a distance, but now all this has been forgotten, since he is finally happily in love with a woman who is real. Although the pastor tries to distinguish fantasy from reality, he actually fell in love with the same object. Both times, he loved the woman because of something more in her than herself. Since it was always the object *a* in the woman that attracted the pastor, for his love to emerge it did not really matter whether the beloved was a "fantasy" or "reality" – a distant dancer in a Broadway show or an innocent country girl.

But the crucial problem of the story is: why was Lynnete repulsed when she discovered the memento? Why wasn't she happy that she herself was his great past love? One explanation for her horror could be her fear that the pastor might stop loving her if he found out about her deception. However, there is another explanation for Lynnete's repulsion: Lynnete is horrified to encounter the very elusive object of love itself – the object *a*, represented here by the garter. However, for the pastor this object is not only the always elusive object of his desire, but also the object through which he enjoyed. And this creates a problem for Lynnete: she wants to be the object desired by the pastor, but not the object through which he found his particular form of *jouissance*.

This story can help us understand the universal dilemma of neurotics, which has to do with the subject's desire to be desired by another subject, while he or she does not want to be the object through which another enjoys.[22] Returning to the story of Odysseus and the Sirens, it can be said that Odysseus actually desires the Sirens (and maybe even wants to be desired by them); however, what causes problems for him is the peculiar way the Sirens enjoy.

HOW DO THE SIRENS ENJOY?

Odysseus' encounter with the Sirens must be understood as a failure. However we read this encounter, as the seduction of Odysseus by the Sirens or vice versa, whatever attraction existed between them never brought the two parties together. That Odysseus escaped the Sirens is commonly understood as his triumph; however, it can also be understood as his failure to confront and pursue his desire. This failed encounter between Odysseus and the Sirens can also be taken as the prototype of the impossibility of the sexual relationship between men and women.

A man falls in love with a woman because he perceives in her something that she actually does not have, the object *a*, the object cause of desire. He will therefore fall in love with a woman because of some particularity – her smile, some gesture, her hair or the tone of her voice, whatever will fill the place of the object *a* for him. And around this object a man will form the fantasy scenario that will enable him to stay in love. The problem for a woman is that she knows very well that a man will fall in love with her because of some particularity that distinguishes her from other women and, as a result, she will desperately try to enhance what she thinks is special about herself. However, a woman can never predict just what particularity will make a man fall in love with her. Thus, one woman might nurture her beautiful lips, thinking that men are attracted by her sensual smile; meanwhile, a man does fall in love with her, but mainly because of her fairly unattractive voice. It is needless to point out that the whole cosmetic and fashion industry relies on women's search for the object in themselves that makes them the object of love. And since women can never guess what is more in them than themselves, the fashion industry encourages them to continue looking for another product that would make them unique.[23]

In Lacan's formulas of sexual difference, a man is totally determined by the phallic function; however, there is one man, the Freudian primordial father, who is the exception. As the possessor of all the women, he is also the one who prohibits other men's access to women. This father of the primal horde is the only one who has direct access to sexual *jouissance* and for whom there is no prohibition against incest. The sexuality of other men is essentially linked to prohibition; they have undergone symbolic castration, after which they are not able to enjoy the body of the woman as a whole.

It is wrong to understand castration as something that prevents the subject's rapport with the opposite sex. After the subject has undergone castration, he or she will not be able to engage in simple animal copulation, i.e. heterosexual intercourse will cease to be an instinctual activity linked to the preservation of the species. However, with humans, castration should not be understood as the basis for denying the possibility of the sexual relation, but as the prerequisite for any sexual relation at all. It can even be said that it is only because subjects are castrated that human relations as such can exist. Castration enables the subject to take others as Other rather than the same, since it is only after undergoing symbolic castration that the subject becomes preoccupied with questions such as: "What does the Other want?" and "What am I for the Other?"[24]

Why is men's symbolic castration crucial to their love liaisons with women? The fact that a man is totally subjected to the phallic function means that he is marked by a lack. After being barred by language, a man will endlessly deal with two questions: first, what is my symbolic identity?[25] (i.e. who am I in the symbolic network?), and second, what object can complement me? The subject deals with this second question in his love life when he searches for the object in the woman, which would enable him to form the fantasy of an always provisional wholeness. When encountering his love-object, a man will want to know what kind of symbolic role the woman sees him in. In contrast to the woman's problem of wondering what kind of object she is for the Other, a man's concern is whether the woman recognizes his symbolic authority. Here a man's obsessions with social status, wealth, prestige all play an important part. This throws a new light on the example from Chabrol's film analyzed in Chapter 1. The millionaire's comment, that he is tired of women insisting that they love him for what he is and that he would like to meet a woman who would finally love him for his millions, can be understood as a confirmation that a man wants to be loved for what is in him that is more than himself – his symbolic status. Although a man has access only to phallic *jouissance*, he nonetheless has aspirations to the Other's *jouissance*, i.e. to the *jouissance* that is beyond the limits of the phallus. This aspiration is paradoxically caused by the superego's command to enjoy, which arouses the man's thirst for the infinity of the Other, while at the same time prohibiting access to it.

The paradox of the superego is that, on the one hand, it is linked to the law of castration (because of which man's *jouissance* can only be phallic); but, on the other hand, the superego is also a command that goes beyond any law. In sum: the superego is analogous to castration in its prohibitive function, while at the same time it has not submitted to the phallic order.[26] As a result, the superego is a demonic agency that commands the subject to go beyond the phallic order and to experience a non-phallic *jouissance*, but such an agency also prohibits the subject access to this *jouissance*. That is why the superego is like the laughing voice of the primordial father, who appears to be saying to the son: "Now that you have killed me, go and finally enjoy women, but you will see that you are actually unable to do so; thus, it is better that you not even try."

When Lacan speaks about feminine *jouissance* he emphasizes the impossibility of defining what it is. Since women are also determined by the phallic function, feminine *jouissance* is not something that women have instead of phallic *jouissance*, but in addition to it. Feminine *jouissance* is thus a supplement to phallic *jouissance*: while the man has access to only one form of *jouissance*, the woman has access to another, additional *jouissance*. Lacan points out that feminine *jouissance* is only a potentiality for women, since women do not expect it. And the woman knows nothing more about this *jouissance* than the simple fact that she enjoys it. She does not talk about it, since it is something inaccessible to language.

A man tries to find out what feminine *jouissance* is: he may even hope to experience it himself, but he always fails in these attempts. For Lacan, such failure is analogous to Achilles' failure to match the speed of the tortoise: she is either ahead of him or already overtaken.[27] In the psychoanalytic clinic, this failure is embodied in the two most common male sexual problems: premature or late ejaculation.

In this context, how can we read the story of Odysseus' encounter with the Sirens and his silence about the Sirens' song? In the *Odyssey*, we have on the one hand, a promise of a limitless *jouissance* in the form of the Sirens' song, and, on the other hand, a prohibition against ever hearing this song. This promise in the Sirens' song can be understood as linked to Odysseus' superego: whatever voice Odysseus hears might be nothing but the voice of his superego, which commands him to experience feminine *jouissance*. But this voice also warns Odysseus of the deadliness of such *jouissance* and thus prohibits his access to it.

However, this explanation does not address the question of whether the Sirens actually did sing. Even if Odysseus heard nothing but his superego's voice, the Sirens might still have been singing. But the question remains: did the Sirens want to be heard by Odysseus, i.e. did they need him as an audience? Since the Sirens' song embodies the ultimate myth of feminine *jouissance*, the question is also whether women need men in order to experience this *jouissance*? The Lacan of the sixties hinted at a positive answer to this question, when he said that a man acts as the relay whereby the woman becomes the Other to herself, as she is the Other for the man.[28] But in later years, Lacan complicates matters when in the seminar *Encore*, he claims that the woman does not necessarily need a man to experience feminine *jouissance*, since she is in a specific way self-sufficient in it. A woman might experience feminine *jouissance* simply by herself, or in a mystical experience, by relating to God.

How can we understand this self-sufficiency of women? Let us take the case of a *femme fatale*, usually perceived as a woman who desperately tries to impress men, who masquerades in order to be admired by men. But a *femme fatale* also has a certain ignorance about men, and it is this very ignorance that actually makes her so attractive. Freud pointed out that the ignorance of the *femme fatale*, as well as of young children and wild cats, is related to the fact that they have not given up on some part of their libido: since other people have lost this libido, they become extremely attracted to those who still retain some of it. The paradox of the *femme fatale*, therefore, is that she wants to be admired for her beauty, but she is perceived as beautiful precisely because she is also ignorant about others' reaction to her. A *femme fatale* enjoys her own self-sufficiency, which is why we cannot simply say that she needs men as relays to her *jouissance*. Of course, she wants to catch and hold the gaze of men, but she is attractive because she quickly turns around and shows very little interest in her admirers.

HOMER WITH KAFKA

We can take the Sirens as such *femmes fatales*, creatures who enjoy their singing and because of this *jouissance* are admired by sailors: although the Sirens encourage the sailors to stop and listen to them, they possess a certain self-sufficiency and will never express more than a fleeting interest in the passing ships. Such a reading remains within the confines of the standard sexualized opposition between masculine desire and feminine drive: men are actively engaged in penetrating the enigma of the Other's desire, while the fundamental feminine attitude is that of drive's closed self-sufficiency – in short, men are subjects, while women are objects. But what if we imagine an alternative version of Odysseus' adventure with the Sirens, in which the agents reverse their respective roles, i.e. in which Odysseus, a being of self-sufficient drive, confronts Sirens, feminine subjects of desire? In his short essay on the "Silence of the Sirens", Franz Kafka accomplished this reversal. His starting point is that the measures that Odysseus and his sailors took to protect themselves from the Sirens' song were simply childish, since it was well known that nothing can protect men from the Sirens' allure. Although it is said that no one survives an encounter with the Sirens, Kafka speculates that "it is conceivable that someone might possibly have escaped from their singing; but from their silence never".[29] Now, what happened when Odysseus approached the Sirens? Kafka's answer is that during this encounter, the potent songstresses actually did not sing, whether because they thought that this enemy could be vanquished only by their silence, or because the look of bliss on the face of [Odysseus], who was thinking of nothing but his wax and his chains, made them forget their singing. But [Odysseus], if one may so express it, did not hear their silence; he thought they were singing and that he alone did not hear them.[30]

In short, Odysseus was so absorbed in himself that he did not notice that the Sirens did not sing. Kafka's guess is that for a fleeting moment Odysseus saw them and from the movements of their throats, their lips half-parted and their eyes filled with tears, he concluded that they were actually singing: "Soon however, all this faded from his sight as he fixed his gaze on the distance, the Sirens literally vanished before his resolution, and at the very moment when they were nearest to him he knew of them no longer."[31] Kafka goes on to speculate that "they – lovelier than ever – stretched their necks and turned, let their cold hair flutter free in the wind, and forgetting everything clung with their claws to the rocks. They no longer had any desire to allure; all they wanted was to hold as long as they could the radiance that fell from [Odysseus'] great eyes."[32]

Kafka thus reinterprets the encounter between the Sirens and Odysseus by claiming that the Sirens themselves became fascinated by Odysseus and not vice versa. Many misperceptions are at work in the encounter; the first is that Odysseus does not notice that the Sirens are actually silent. This misperception makes him overconfident in his strength, which also makes him ignorant about the Sirens, and his ignorance induces the Sirens to become enchanted by his gaze. The second misperception is that the Sirens do not notice that Odysseus' gaze is not directed toward them at all. The failed encounter between the Sirens and Odysseus can thus be summarized: that Odysseus does not notice that the Sirens are silent, but thinks he has mastered their voice, makes his gaze so alluring in its self-confidence that the Sirens fall desperately in love with him.

Kafka's re-reading of the *Odyssey* can easily be understood as a myth endeavouring to restore men to their dominant position: a man does not perish when encountering a seductive, monstrous female, if he reverses the situation and induces the female to fall in love with him. If some stories say that the Sirens committed suicide when they failed to enchant Odysseus, Kafka offers an even more devastating account of their lack of power: because they fall in love with Odysseus, they are unable even to sing. We meet a similar situation in Kafka's "Before the Law", where the man learns at the end of the story that the doors of the law were closed only against him. He is thus not a nobody before the law: the whole legal spectacle was carried out just for him. The same goes for Kafka's Odysseus: he is not just one of the many sailors who pass by the Sirens' island; he is the one, and the only one, that the Sirens are interested in.

Kafka's reinterpretation of Odysseus' story enacts Lacan's notion of the magic moment of reversal of the loved one into the loving subject, which was analyzed in the last chapter. The relationship between Odysseus and the Sirens can also be taken as a myth of the two hands: one hand (the hand of the desiring subject) extends itself and tries to attract the beautiful object (the loved object immersed in the self-sufficiency of drive), while suddenly another hand emerges from the site of the object and touches the first one, i.e. the object of love returns love, turns into a loving subject.[33] But why does the unification of the two hands actually fail to take place? The answer is very simple in its compelling necessity and is beautifully enacted in Kafka's version: at that very moment, the first subject no longer notices the hand reaching back, since he himself now turns into a self-sufficient being of drive. Kafka's Sirens lose their self-sufficiency when they subjectivize themselves by falling in love with Odysseus, and they fall mute as a result.

The crucial question here is: do the Sirens give up on their *jouissance* when they subjectivize themselves? If, for Kafka, this subjectivization results in muteness; for other post-Homerian interpreters, the subjectivization of the Sirens is linked to their recognition that they have failed to seduce Odysseus; as a result, they commit suicide. It would be wrong to take the muteness of the Sirens or their suicide as proof that they have given up on their *jouissance* as the result of their subjectivization. Although the Sirens may have subjectivized themselves, they still persist in their deadly *jouissance*. That the Sirens either become mute or die proves that they did not compromise their *jouissance*. Was it not Freud himself who associated drives with a fundamental *silence*, claiming that they pursue their work *silently*, outside the resonating space of the public word? Had the Sirens compromised their *jouissance*, they would have become "ordinary" women who would have tried to pursue Odysseus. But then they would never have gained the status of mythical figures.

The reversal of roles between the Sirens and Odysseus in Kafka is thus not quite symmetrical, since there is a crucial difference between the way the Sirens are subjectivized and the way Odysseus is subjectivized in his fascination with the enigma of the Sirens' song (in the standard version of the story). Odysseus did give up on his *jouissance* (which is why he was able to talk, to remember his experience, to enter the domain of intersubjective community), while the Sirens' silence bears witness to the fact that, precisely, *they refused to do this*. What the Sirens' silence offers is an exemplary case of *subjectivization without accepting symbolic castration* (the Lacanian name for this gesture of giving up on one's *jouissance*). Perhaps this paradox of a subjectivity which nonetheless rejects the phallic economy of the symbolic castration defines the central feature of the feminine subject. And my point is not that Kafka merely gives a modernist twist to the standard version of the encounter between Odysseus and the Sirens. In a much more radical way, Kafka's reversal provides the *truth* of the standard version: the reversal described by Kafka *was always already operative* in the standard version of the myth as its disavowed background. Odysseus fascinated with the presubjectivized lethal song of the Sirens, intent on probing its secret – is this not the myth of male desire, sustained by the reality of the male subject enamored in his own fantasmatic formation and, for this reason, ignorant of the invisible, but persistent feminine subjectivity?

NOTES

1. Various stories explain why the Sirens became half-bird and half-woman. Ovid relates that they were once ordinary girls, companions of Persephone. When she was abducted by Pluto, they asked the gods for wings to help them in their search for their companion. Other authors attribute this transformation to the anger of Demeter, since the Sirens failed to prevent the abduction of her daughter. It was also said that Aphrodite deprived them of their beauty because they scorned the pleasures of love. After their transformation from humans to half-birds they tried to rival the Muses, who then removed all their feathers. (See Pierre Grimal, *Dictionary of Classical Mythology*, Harmondsworth, Middx: Penguin 1991, p. 403.)
2. Jean-Pierre Vernant, *Mortals and Immortals: Collected Essays*, ed. Froma I. Zeitlin, Princeton, NJ: Princeton University Press 1991, p. 104.
3. Homer, *The Odyssey*, trans. Robert Fagles, New York: Viking Penguin 1996, p. 272.
4. Some theorists claim that the idea of the Sirens came from the bee-cult that existed in the pre-Hellenic Mediterranean and which associated bees with various goddesses, as well as with the spirits of the dead. See Gabriel

Germain, "The Sirens and the Temptation of Knowledge", in *Homer: A Collection of Critical Essays*, ed. George Steiner and Robert Fagles, Englewood Cliffs, NJ: Prentice-Hall 1963.

5. Homer, *Odyssey*, p. 277.

6. For Pietro Pucci, this forceful representation of enchantment is unique in world literature, comparable only to Plato's portrayal of Alcibiades' cursed subjugation to Socrates' beguiling discourse. See Pietro Pucci, *Odysseus Polutropos: Intertextual Readings in the Odyssey and the Iliad*, Ithaca, NY: Cornell University Press 1987, p. 210.

7. Here, Pucci claims that "the text of the Sirens' invitation and promise . . . is 'written' in strictly Iliadic diction" (ibid., footnote 7).

8. Ibid., p. 212.

9. Ibid.

10. Tzvetan Todorov, *The Poetics of Prose*, trans. Richard Howard, Oxford: Basil Blackwell 1977, pp. 58–9. Maurice Blanchot also analyzes Odysseus' encounter with the Sirens as the problem of narration. However, Blanchot's thesis is that Odysseus actually heard the Sirens, but "with the disturbing deafness of he who is deaf because he hears". Odysseus "took no risks but admired the Sirens with the cowardly, unemotional, calculated satisfaction characteristic of the decadent Greek he was who should never have figured among the heroes of the Iliad". See Maurice Blanchot, "The Sirens' Song", in *Selected Essays by Maurice Blanchot*, ed. Gabriel Josipovici, trans. Sacha Rabinovich, Brighton, Sussex: Harvester Press 1982, p. 60.

11. The Muses are "supreme in their fields, and those who dare challenge them meet with defeat and punishment". See Mark P.O. Monford and Robert J. Lenadron, *Classical Mythology*, London: Longman 1991, p. 88.

12. Robert Graves, *The Greek Myths*, vol. 2, Harmondsworth: Penguin 1990, pp. 281, 282. "Hesiod claimed that they accompany kings and inspire them with the persuasive words necessary to settle quarrels and re-establish peace, and give kings the gentleness which makes them dear to their subjects" (ibid.).

13. Charles Segal, *Singers, Heroes and Gods in the Odyssey*, Ithaca: Cornell University Press 1994, p. 103. There are also claims that forgetfulness comes to the men who listen to the Sirens' song. George B. Walsh thus says that "the Sirens' song is deadly in its charm, apparently because it brings men so much pleasure they forget to live". See his *The Varieties of Enchantment: Early Greek Views of the Nature and Function of Poetry*, Chapel Hill: University of North Carolina Press 1984, p. 15.

14. Jacques Lacan, *The Four Fundamental Concepts of Psycho-Analysis*, trans. Alan Sheridan, New York: Norton 1977, p. 49.

15. Max Horkheimer and Theodor W. Adorno, *Dialectic of Enlightenment*, trans. John Cumming, New York: Seabury Press 1986, pp. 32, 33. In contrast, Bertolt Brecht takes the Sirens' singing as art, but he questions

whether these divine singers would really waste their talents by singing for ordinary people. See "Berichtigungen alter Mythen", in Bertolt Brecht, *Prosa*, Band 1, Berlin: Aufbau Verlag 1973, p. 200.

16. For a detailed Lacanian account of voice, see Mladen Dolar, "The Object Voice", in *Gaze and Voice as Love Objects*, ed. Renata Salecl and Slavoj Žižek, Durham: Duke University Press 1996.

17. Michel Poizat, *The Angel's Cry*, Ithaca, NY: Cornell University Press 1992, p. 35.

18. Ibid.

19. Jacques Lacan, *Ecrits: A Selection*, trans. Alan Sheridan, New York: Norton 1977, p. 321.

20. Ibid., p. 270.

21. See Juan-Carlos Indart, "Etude d'un symptôme obsessionnel", *Ornicar?* 28 (Paris 1984).

22. Here, of course, perverts differ from neurotics, since they want to be the object of the Other's *jouissance*. However, in this case, the pervert actually imposes a specific form of *jouissance* on the Other.

23. It is significant that women's journals, which are usually greatly influenced by cosmetic and fashion corporations, advise women whose husbands cheat to buy new clothes, especially lingerie, to make themselves the object of love again. We can agree with the German designer Joop that designer shops today function as places for therapy. The failure of the fashion industry to find the object that would satisfy the consumers' desire helps this industry to flourish, but it also helps psychoanalysts to stay in business, since traumas usually cannot be resolved by simply buying a new dress.

24. That human sexuality undergoes symbolic castration means that so-called natural sexuality or even animality is repressed when the subject becomes the being of language. Repression also means that something in the subject becomes sexualized that hasn't been before, i.e. the function of repression is to make a sexual reality out of the real. (See Jacques Lacan, *On Feminine Sexuality: The Limits of Love and Knowledge (Book XX – Encore 1972–1973)*, trans. Bruce Fink, New York: Norton 1998.)

   Repression thus contributes to the fact that with the subject the partial objects like gaze, voice or breast become sexualized and function as objects of drive. Since the subject has no genital drive, these other objects play a more crucial role in the subject's sexuality than his or her sexual organs.

25. Men who stutter have problems with their symbolic role. These men do not simply have difficulty in speaking, but rather have difficulty in assuming a position in a symbolic network, i.e. occupying the place from which to speak. Although we usually perceive women as being voiceless in our patriarchal culture, one rarely finds women who stutter, which confirms that women do not experience problems with their symbolic role in the

same way as men. See Darian Leader, *Why Do Women Write More Letters Than They Post?*, London: Faber and Faber 1996, pp. 127–8.

26. Geneviève Morel, "L'hypothèse de compacité et les logiques de la succession dans le chapitre I d'Encore", in *La Cause Freudienne* 25 (1993), p. 102.

27. See Jacques Lacan, *On Feminine Sexuality*, p. 8. See also Serge André, *Que veut une femme?*, Paris: Editions du Seuil 1995.

28. Jacques Lacan, "Guiding Remarks for a Congress on Feminine Sexuality", in *Feminine Sexuality: Jacques Lacan and the Ecole Freudienne*, ed. Juliet Mitchell and Jacqueline Rose, London: Macmillan 1982, p. 93.

29. Franz Kafka, "The Silence of the Sirens", in *Homer: A Collection of Critical Essays*, ed. George Steiner and Robert Fagles, Englewood Cliffs, NJ: Prentice-Hall 1963, p. 98.

30. Ibid.

31. Ibid.

32. Ibid., p. 99.

33. Jacques Lacan, *Le Séminaire, livre VIII: Le transfert*, Paris: Editions du Seuil 1991, p. 67.

4

FOR THE LOVE OF THE NATION: CEAUŞESCU'S DISNEYLAND

Passionate attachments not only affect people's private lives, they can also torment a whole nation. There are always grounds for concern when politicians declare their love for their country, since this love can be extremely destructive. When the former East Germany was in the process of disintegration, Erich Mielke, the head of State Security, defended himself from opposition attacks by claiming: "But I love you all." And when at Ceauşescu's last public rally the crowd started shouting at him, he also extended his hands in a fatherly way as if to embrace it. Ceauşescu was displaying his love for the Romanian people, but his was an especially destructive kind of love. During his long rule, he not only imposed strong ideological control over the country and brought it to extreme poverty, he physically ruined the center of Bucharest and destroyed numerous old villages to realize communist ideals in the organization of public spaces. Ceauşescu's relation to Romania seemed to follow the logic: "I love my country, but since I love in my country something more than it, I mutilate it." This notion "in my country more than the country itself" was the nationalist communist ideal, the true object of Ceauşescu's passionate attachment; and to bring reality closer to this ideal, he made enormous cuts in the "flesh" of the country.

People living in post-communist countries have great difficulty in deciding what to do with communist monuments and the other physical remnants of the past regime. Meanwhile, they also try to come to terms with their memory of the past, and some even feel nostalgic about the old days. How can one understand such nostalgia for a totalitarian past?

The well-known communist joke inquires: "What is the difference between an optimist and a pessimist in the Soviet Union?" "A pessimist thinks that everything is so bad that it can't get worse, while an optimist thinks that it can." Nowadays, many Russians and other east Europeans still hold such an "optimistic" view, confronted as they are with the economic chaos of early capitalism which makes their lives even more difficult than they were under the communist regime. Some people feel a deep despair and daydream about past times, when there was less freedom but more social security.[1] For them, the fall of communism was an event that brought disarray to their lives. Clinging to this perception, they act like hysterics who always find a point in their symbolic economy, a particular event, that instigated their suffering. Such a hysteric usually concludes: "If only my mother hadn't done this in my youth ... if only that encounter had never occurred ... if only I could turn the clock backwards and arrange things differently." Belief in such an "if only" is a necessary fantasy that enables the hysteric to sustain the position of innocent victim. Since the clock cannot be turned back, the hysteric can do nothing to change the situation.

So it is for those who are nostalgic about communism: since it belongs irretrievably in the past, they do not need to act to improve their current situation. That is why the vast majority of such people do not engage in serious political struggle; they do not organize political parties that would, for example, campaign for a return to communism. Instead, they persist in the comfortable role of the lamenting victim.[2] The paradox is that in the past, they wished for the end of communism, but they did not truly believe that their wish could be fulfilled. And today they act in a similar fashion when they dream about returning to the safe shelter of communist institutions, while knowing that this cannot happen. In their attitude toward the unattainable past, these nostalgic men and women greatly resemble the disenchanted lovers analyzed in Chapter 1, who mourn for lost love and at the same time do everything to prevent the realization of their desire.

People's nostalgia for the past poses a variety of theoretical questions: how is the identity of the subject related to the symbolic order and which memory of the past does the subject invoke? Since this past never existed in the way it is now remembered, what is the logic of this memory? In the case of communist nostalgia, questions also arise about how the new regime should deal with the visible monuments of the previous one (communist statues, architecture, etc.), and what it means to remove them or to integrate them into the post-socialist ideological universe. But, in order to answer this last question, it is necessary to understand why these monuments were built in the first place. In the case of Ceauşescu, for example, the question is: what was the nature of his passionate attachment to communist ideals that required the destruction of the country?

IDENTITY AND INSTITUTION

Certain prisoners serving life sentences display an impossible desire: they dream endlessly about "freedom", but when they are eventually released, they nostalgically remember the "non-freedom" of their prison life. This impossible desire is a major theme of the movie *The Shawshank Redemption* (Frank Darabont, 1994), based on a short story by Stephen King. In the film, the prisoner Red, serving a life sentence, narrates a story about another lifer, Andy, a young banker, convicted of murdering his wife and her lover. Andy is a special person: he radiates a certain calm, as if the horror of prison does not touch him in his inner being. In contrast, other prisoners are, as Red says, "institutionalized men": their identity depends on the place they have in the prison hierarchy. When released from prison, they become broken individuals who either commit another crime in order to be reincarcerated or decide to end their lives. Andy claims that he is innocent; however, he does not perceive himself as a suffering victim, but stoically endures the oppression of prison. His one particularity is that he always has a big poster hanging in his cell: first of Rita Hayworth, then Marilyn Monroe and later various other beauties. When, after nineteen years of prison life, Andy suddenly disappears, it becomes clear that this poster hid a large hole in the wall, by which he had slowly dug himself out of prison and finally escaped.

At this point, Andy's story ends and the focus turns to Red himself, who after thirty-eight years is unexpectedly paroled. Red knows that he too is an "institutionalized man" and that life outside has no meaning, but what prevents him from collapsing is the example of Andy. (Here the film version and the short story differ slightly.) In the film, the prisoner Andy had once asked Red to do him a favor: if and when Red is released, he is to seek a field in Maine where something is hidden under a black stone. Andy directly encourages Red to search for a secret, thus giving him hope, an object of desire. In the original short story, the search for this object is more profound. Andy reveals to Red his own plan, after getting out of prison, to find a black rock under which lies a key to a bank safe. In this safe, a friend has stored bonds and documents for Andy's new identity, which will enable him to start a new life in Mexico. In the original story, it is essential that Andy does not directly encourage Red to find the secret under the black rock, but only reveals his (Andy's) own object of desire.

Since "desire is always desire of the Other", the notion of the secret rock quickly becomes Red's own obsession. Red, when released, starts searching for the field in Maine and discovers the rock and its secret: a letter from Andy addressed to him. In this letter, Andy encourages Red: since he has come so far, he can go even farther and join him in Mexico: "Remember, hope is a good thing."[3]

For convicts, the jail sentence does not simply involve an agonizing ordeal; they find a special enjoyment in their suffering. The point is not that they take pleasure in grumbling about the injustice of the jail sentence. What is essential is how, in the oppressiveness of the prison situation, the prisoners organize their identities. The convicts enjoy establishing internal rules, forming hierarchies, humiliating each other and pitting one inmate against another. The prison thus provides a ground on which each prisoner forms his identity, either as one who knows how to work the rules, climbs in the hierarchy and masters the others, or as one who is endlessly victimized by his peers.

How is one to understand this notion of identity? Those theorists who conceive of identity in terms of subject positions insist that it is primarily linked to the problem of intersubjectivity. The subject's identity thus depends on his or her relationship to the Other, in the sense of the social symbolic structure as well as the concrete other subject. In the case of prisoners, an individual's identity is determined by the place he or she occupies in relation to the symbolic organization of the prison, as well as to the other prisoners. Lacan, however, would go further: for him identity is the way the subject deals with his or her radical lack. By taking on a symbolic identity, by identifying with a place in the social symbolic network, the subject tries to avoid the encounter with this lack, the unsymbolizable real that determines the subject in his or her inner being. The subject thus searches for places in various social hierarchies in order to escape the trauma of the real.

In the prison situation, the real relates to the crime in a specific way. In the wider social world, crime is the real around which the law establishes itself (or according to Hegel, out of which the law emerges as the negation of crime). However, crime is also what the law tries to encompass, but what nonetheless always escapes its grasp. The crime committed by the subject destroys the subject's former identity, since it also touches the unsymbolizable kernel, the lack around which the subject structures his or her identity. Thus, after committing the crime, the subject will never be the same again; he or she will never form his or her identity in the same way as before. The new identity the subject forms in prison thus has to do with the real (related to) crime, or better, this identity enables the subject to escape this real. That is why, as the film clearly shows, the prisoners do not talk about their crimes, they do not boast about their murders: they all claim that they are innocent and that their conviction was a horrible mistake. They do this not because they are sorry for their past deeds: what is more in the prisoner than he himself, that which makes him a convict – the crime – has to remain hidden, unspoken, in order that he can form his new symbolic identity.

The identity of the prisoner is thus primarily linked to an unspeakable crime, the real; however, it also relates to the perception of the unattainable "freedom" on the other side of the bars. But for many prisoners attaining this "freedom" causes total collapse – the loss of all they had: their identity breaks down when they come out. In King's story, the prototype of such a broken prisoner is the old librarian Brooks, who commits suicide when the authorities release him from prison in his old age: "He was crying when he left. Shawshank was his world. What lay beyond its walls was as terrible to Brooks as the Western Seas had been to superstitious fifteenth-century sailors. In prison, Brooksie had been a person of some importance. He was the librarian, an educated man. If he went to the Kittery library and asked for a job, they wouldn't even give him a library card."[4] How does one become such an "institutionalized man"? As Red contemplates: "At first you can't stand those four walls, then you get so you can abide them, then you get so you accept them . . . and then, as your body and your mind and your spirit adjust to life on an HO scale, you get to love them."[5]

But what is the difference between Andy and other prisoners? Andy, although the only truly innocent prisoner, takes the prison rituals seriously. On the surface, he submits to the rules, but meanwhile undermines the institution of the prison from the inside. (Andy "undermines" not only the wall in his prison cell, but also the illegal financial businesses of the prison authorities.) Despite performing the rituals and accepting prison as a necessary evil, Andy does not organize his identity around prison. He decides upon a goal, the object of his desire – opening a hotel in Mexico – around which he then organizes his life by slowly plotting his escape. It is this object of desire – in Andy's terms "hope" – that gives him a special freedom.[6] The other prisoners, in contrast, do not take the rituals seriously, they constantly complain about them and try in every way to evade coercion. But paradoxically, the institution holds on to them precisely at the point when they think that it will lose control over them forever – the moment of their release. While Andy submits to the rituals externally but not in his inner self, for the other prisoners it is the other way around: they rebel against the constraints of prison, but the institution has a hold on them from the inside. And when the external coercion, against which they rebelled, ceases to exist, their world collapses. As old Red recognizes, once outside of prison, he cannot even go to the toilet, since for so many years he was used to going on orders.

During the long years of digging his escape tunnel, Andy was not sure whether he could realize his desire, but by slowly progressing with his work on the hole, he organized a ritual that kept his desire in motion. The turning point for him came when he realized that the hole could actually lead to freedom: "All at once he must have realized that, instead of just playing a game, he was playing for high stakes . . . in terms of his own life, and his own future, the highest . . . All of a sudden, instead of just being a toy, that stupid hole in the wall became his master."[7] But Andy does not collapse at this point, he does not "lose his head" – the object of his desire does not "swallow" him when it becomes attainable. On the contrary, since Andy obeys the ritual and his object of desire is subordinated to the symbolic order, he retains his "normality". Once on the outside, he again organizes his ritual, building a hotel and finding a new goal. Andy's freedom is thus always subordinated to some ritual, to some discipline, while for the other prisoners, freedom itself is their object of desire: what they desire is to get out, and suppose that attaining this goal will change everything for the better. However, when they obtain freedom, it destroys them, since the structure that kept their object of desire – freedom – at bay, i.e. subordinated to the ritual of prison, ceases to exist.

In King's story, what keeps Red alive is identification with Andy as his Ego Ideal. Through this identification, Red organizes another ritual – the search for the secret object of Andy's desire – that keeps his own desire in motion. The fact that desire is always desire of the Other means that desire has to be subordinated to the symbolic order, while remaining a striving for something else, something that the symbolic order cannot encompass. Thus, Red can say: "Andy was the part of me they could never lock up, the part of me that will rejoice when the gates finally open for me."[8] But this identification with Andy also enables Red to find another institution when the penal one ceases to exist.

Under socialism, people whose stance toward communist institutions resembled Andy's attitude toward prison were not traumatized because of their confinement within totalitarianism, but were slowly undermining the regime itself. Their identification with the regime was on the surface, but it did not touch their inner being. For these people, their world did not collapse when the system disintegrated and they lost the security of the oppressive institution. In contrast, those who looked back nostalgically to the past were the real "institutionalized men", who constantly criticized the institutions, but whose identity fully relied on them. Now, these two types differ first in their "crime" and second in their perception of the institution. Under socialism, in the eyes of the Party, everyone was potentially guilty of some crime (not believing in the regime, petty theft at the workplace, bribery, etc.). But this was not the guilt that really traumatized people; another, more horrible guilt was that most people collaborated in some way or another with the regime (they denounced their colleagues to save their own skins, they did not oppose injustices when they should have, or they simply kept quiet).[9] And it was guilt for this "crime" that essentially determined their identification with the system. People did not consciously identify with the regime, but formed their identities around the trauma of their guilt. Implicated in this way, they passively criticized the system without ever endangering its foundations. In contrast, the "socialist Andys" were those dissidents who did not get trapped in this circle of guilt. They also did not believe that "freedom" existed outside the institution. Their undermining of the socialist regime did not try to achieve ultimate freedom; instead, it aimed to produce a different kind of institution – possibly a more democratic one.

THE NOSTALGIA OF MEMORY

Thus, in order to escape the traumatic kernel in his or her inner being, the subject endlessly searches for some point of identification with the symbolic order that would give him or her a place in the social structure – which means the promise of an identity. When this attempt fails, what remains is the memory of some "happy before" when everything was "different". What is the logic of this memory?

With his famous concept of "screen memories" (*Deckerinnerung*), Freud showed how the subject usually produces some quite irrelevant memory to cover up something he or she does not want to remember. Thus, what is important remains suppressed and what is insignificant is retained in the subject's memory. For Freud:

> What is recorded in the memory is not the relevant experience itself – in this respect the resistance gets its way; what is recorded is another psychical element closely associated with the objectionable one – and in this respect the first principle shows its strength, the principle which endeavors to fix important impressions by establishing reproducible memory pictures. The result of the conflict is therefore that, instead of the memory which would have been justified by the original event, another memory is produced which has been by some degree associatively displaced from the former one.[10]

The subject produces this displaced memory in order to avoid the trauma of another memory, so that the coherence of the story that the subject tells him or herself is not shattered.

In a social context, such displacement of cultural memory goes on continuously. In Slovenia, one example is the Christian Democrats' attempt to extend maternity leave to up to three years, which they claim is necessary to increase the very low birth rate, solve unemployment and, above all, grant children the right to parental care during the first crucial years of life. To bring the public round to their view, the Christian Democrats have invoked the image of happy family life as it supposedly existed in the past, when people lived in rural communities, in extended family households, where children had the love and attention of their parents, and where mothers were not employed and could devote themselves fully to each child's upbringing. Of course, this happy family never existed. The memory that is repressed is the memory of parental indifference or even violence, which was what actually characterized pre-modern family life. In the past, children in rural areas were mostly perceived as a much needed workforce and were treated very badly: as babies, their arms and legs were swaddled so that they could not move, they were given alcohol to stifle their crying, they ate with the servants, etc. Paradoxically, this violence tends to be completely forgotten in the rightists' nostalgia for the past.

For Lacan, memory primarily has to do with not remembering the trauma, the real on which the subject centers his or her very being. When we tell our stories, it is the point at which we touch the real that our words fail, but fail so as to always come back to the trauma without being able to articulate it. As Lacan says:

The subject in himself, the recalling of his biography, all this goes only to a certain limit, which is known as the real ... An adequate thought, *qua* thought, at the level at which we are, always avoids – if only to find itself again later in everything – the same thing. Here the real is that which always comes back to the same place – to the place where the subject, in so far as he thinks, where the *res cogitans*, does not meet it.[11]

Thus one can imagine that prisoners who do not talk about their crime and insist on their innocence occasionally bury their memory of it: in their thoughts, they try to avoid encountering the trauma, only to find that it returns in the unconscious.

The subject, therefore, forms memory in order to obtain certainty, to fashion a story that grants him or her a perception of wholeness – his or her identity. But it can also be said that one remembers so that the social symbolic structure stays fully in its place. Freud's early hysterical patients were very convincing in their remembering. But as Lacan points out: "What is at issue in this remembering could not be known at the outset – one did not know that the desire of the hysteric was the desire of the father, to be sustained in its status. It was hardly surprising that, for the benefit of him who takes the place of the father, one remembered things right down to the dregs."[12] As Chapter 1 showed, the main problem of the hysteric is: what does she represent for the big Other, what kind of an object is she for the big Other? By seeking an answer to this question, the hysteric tries to overcome the constitutive lack that bars her as a subject. For the hysteric, the search for the "father figure" is a way to find confirmation of her own identity. This search also includes a demand for the "father figure" not to be barred. But the impossibility of this demand forces the hysteric to search endlessly for new authority, new "father figures".

However, the paradox of the hysteric is that the authority she searches for is also the authority that she herself wants to control. Such an attitude is exemplified by an ex-student of mine who engaged in long debates during my lectures, but at the end of the class said: "Why do you allow me to talk so much in the class? You should stop me and go on with your lecture, since I prefer to listen to you and not to myself." I can imagine that if I had imposed my authority on her and prevented her interruptions, she might have reported me to the department chair, while also saying to him: "What kind of an authority are you when you take your time and patiently listen to such a stupid complaint as mine?"

For the subject, the very process of remembering is, therefore, an attempt to put and keep the big Other firmly in its place, to secure the existence of the symbolic order so that he or she can achieve some certainty about his or her identity.

Nostalgic remembrance of socialism can similarly be understood as an attempt by those living in post-socialist chaos to find some stability, a symbolic order that would grant them their identities. But in this remembrance we also encounter the problem of how to deal with the relics of the past: how should the new regime "erase" the historic memory of the old regime, which is materialized, for example, in communist monuments or architecture?

Here we have to distinguish between two perceptions of the problem, that of the east Europeans themselves and that of the Western media. After the fall of the communist regimes, when east Europeans started removing communist monuments, some Western intellectuals openly criticized this action, since in their perception, destroying the monuments was equivalent to erasing memory. This thesis is presented in the documentary *Disgraced Monuments* (1992), by Mark Lewis and Laura Mulvey, which deals with the removal of communist monuments in Russia. The film compares the way the post-socialists demolish communist monuments with the way the Bolsheviks tore down those of the Tsarist regime. In both cases the pedestal usually remained; only the statue of the hero on top was removed. This comparison of the two regimes implies that the current and former rulers do not differ in how they deal with historical memory and that zealous destruction of the old monuments will not enable society to end its connection with past revolutionary ideology.

A simple answer to such a critique is that no regime comes into power after a more or less violent upheaval without tearing down images of the previous rulers, especially if these rulers are perceived as totalitarian dictators. In a country where the transfer of power occurs democratically, one can easily erect the statue of the new president alongside the statue of the previous one. But in an authoritarian regime, or in a country where a new, hopefully democratic regime replaces a previously totalitarian one, one should not expect this to happen. If we take the case of post-Hitler Germany, one does not expect to see the Führer's pictures in public places, although he is part of the national memory.

The gaze of those Westerners who regard the post-socialist removal of monuments as a barbaric denial of history is not a gaze from a neutral position. Here, one encounters the perception that east Europeans are "different" from Westerners, which means that they are not able to deal with their history in a "civilized" way. On the one hand, it is easy to agree that demolition of monuments is an inadequate way for the public to express its frustrations and that the symbolic remnants of the previous regime cannot easily be swept under the carpet; but, on the other hand, one cannot expect that the simple preservation of monuments would help the new regime to work through the trauma of the previous one.

An interesting idea about how to "save" such monuments was presented by the Russian-American artists Komar and Melamid. In their view, communist monuments should today be assigned some new "useful!" role. Thus, they made candlesticks from busts of Lenin, in order to realize Lenin's desire to enlighten the people; busts of Marx were turned upside down, since this is what he himself had done with Hegel's philosophy; and monumental statues of euphoric revolutionaries were pushed a little over the edge of the pedestal so that their forward-marching feet hung in mid-air, which symbolizes how actual realization of the communist project itself remained up in the air. Komar and Melamid took the communist project seriously and used its art to deal a little less seriously with the deadlocks in memories of the past.

Some of the monuments built under socialism cannot simply be removed or "redecorated" in the Komar–Melamid manner: these are the grandiose constructions of socialist architecture. And the most astounding of such monuments is Ceauşescu's "House of the Republic", which is today called the "People's House".

THE STATE AS A WORK OF ART

In the late seventies, Ceauşescu began his project of rebuilding the center of Bucharest so that architectural reality would properly reflect the greatness of Romanian communism. Bucharest, which used to be called the "Little Paris" of the Balkans, suddenly became a huge building site. Ceauşescu demanded the demolition of almost a quarter of the old town center with its picturesque streets, old churches, monasteries, hospitals, schools, etc.[13] In its place, a new socialist administrative center started to appear, comprising a grandiose palace and a broad avenue with neo-baroque fountains surrounded by neo-classical apartment blocks. Construction progressed very fast: tens of thousands of laborers and hundreds of

Figure 7 Ceauşescu's "House of the Republic".

architects and engineers worked day and night on the project. This rebuilding demanded enormous financial outlay and significantly increased the
economic hardship of the Romanian people. At the time of the collapse of
Ceauşescu's regime, the project had reached its final stage. The question
was: what should be done with this massive architectural venture? Political
debate about the project became heated, centering on the fate of the palace.
Some people insisted that the palace had to be demolished; others proposed
that it become a museum of communist terror; still others suggested that it
be transformed into a casino. The new regime decided to complete the
project and to establish the palace as the site of the new parliament and as
an international congress center (Figure 7). The palace, however, remains
one of the most traumatic remnants of the communist regime. It has a
sublime quality – it is beautiful and horrible at the same time, provoking
both admiration and disgust. But before analyzing today's perception of
the palace, let us try to explain what led Ceauşescu to create it.

    It is common knowledge that Ceauşescu, who had once enjoyed the
support of the people, in the last years of his rule fell into some kind of
psychotic delirium, into an obsession with his own grandeur. He became a
megalomaniac: a king who believed that he was a king. And his architectural
project tried to materialize this megalomania. One explanation for Ceau-

şescu's obsession with changing the architecture of Bucharest is that, once when traveling abroad, he came to realize that he liked neither Western architectural styles, nor socialist architecture. He found something close to his ideal in North Korea, where his friend Kim Il Sung had begun to construct a new administrative center in Phenian. Romania and North Korea were soon in competition to see which could build the more prestigious and grandiose city.[14] But the main difference between the Romanian and Korean administrative centers is that the latter was constructed on empty ground, while Romania had to sacrifice a large part of old Bucharest.[15] What was the purpose of this sacrifice? Why was it necessary to demolish historic buildings, churches, hospitals and schools?

The idea behind this demolition was not only to find space for Ceauşescu's architectural exercises. Had Ceauşescu simply wanted to find a place for his "artistic" creations, he could easily have found some vacant plot outside the city as the site of his dream town. The demolition should be understood as an essential part of his project. It could even be said that the destruction of buildings, the erasure of historical memory, was more important than the construction of the new center. The "wound" Ceauşescu made in the "living flesh of the city", as Romanians tend to characterize the project, has a special symbolic meaning.[16]

Ceauşescu's undertaking should be understood as a *creatio ex nihilo*, an attempt to make something out of nothing, to totally eradicate the previous symbolic order, which had been realized not only in the past political system but also in its material remnants – its architecture. Lacan has linked this *creatio ex nihilo* with the destructive nature of the death drive. The latter is "a creationist sublimation, and it is linked to that structural element which implies that, as soon as we have to deal with anything in the world appearing in the form of the signifying chain, there is somewhere – though certainly outside the natural world – which is the beyond of that chain, the *ex nihilo* on which it is founded and is articulated as such."[17] As pointed out in Chapter 3, the death drive is a drive of destruction that undermines the social symbolic space; however, linked to it is a will to make a new start, a start from the point of nothing. Lacan also points out that the death drive "is to be situated in the historical domain; it is articulated at a level that can only be defined as a function of the signifying chain".[18] History is to be understood here as something we remember, i.e. as something that is registered in the signifying chain and exists only through this chain. Here, one has to take into account the distinction Lacan makes between memory and remembering (*remémoration*). Only the latter "pertains to the order of history", thus: "One mustn't confuse the *history*, in which the unconscious subject inscribes himself, with his *memory*."[19] History is of the order of the symbolic, while memory touches the real, the trauma that resists symbolization.

It could be said that Ceauşescu's intention was to erase history, but in the course of doing so he produced the trauma that now invokes the memory of the lost past. Thus people today recall the "happy" past, the social security of socialism, in order to escape the memory of the trauma. This trauma includes not only Ceauşescu's violence and destruction, it also touches on the passivity that allowed this annihilation to happen. Here again we encounter the "crime" of people too afraid to oppose the regime and the unconscious feeling of guilt that accompanies this non-action.

Ceauşescu's creationism tried to undo the old signifying chain in order to establish a totally new symbolic organization. By razing historical monuments, he aimed to wipe out Romanian national identity, the fantasy structure of the nation that is forged around historic buildings and churches, and then to establish his own version of this identity.

Ceauşescu's architectural madness is revealed most clearly in the way his urban project dealt with the river that runs through the city. For Ceauşescu, the river functioned as a psychotic object that had to be totally controlled, regulated, split into a good and a bad part. Thus he decided to double the riverbed: the river was divided into two, a lower level being the channel for the dirty water, and an upper level the channel for the "proper", clean river. Then, to avoid its intrusion into his scheme – it crossed the main avenue leading to the palace – construction workers covered over a portion of the river. Hence, where one would expect a bridge, the river is simply erased, covered by concrete, which is enhanced by a green and an ornamental fountain.[20]

In general, Ceauşescu's architectural project tried to construct an ideally beautiful artwork by combining elements from various styles. Something similar was recently undertaken by the aforementioned artists Komar and Melamid, who for their project "The People's Choice" designed and conducted a survey in various countries to find out which motives and which colors people perceived as the most "artistic" and which they perceived as ugly. Then, based on their findings, the artists created two pictures: the first incorporates those elements chosen as the most beautiful and the second is a mixture of those elements chosen as the most unappealing. The supposedly ideally beautiful picture is often in blue and green and presents a romantic landscape with trees, animals, clouds, sun, etc. And the supposedly ugly picture mostly consists of modernist triangles in black and red. The picture that is supposed to unite the most beautiful elements looks like a kitsch postcard, while the ugly picture looks like simplistic abstract art. For both pictures, it is essential that their "ideality", the way they try to perfectly embody "beauty" and "ugliness" annihilates their intended esthetic effect and produces a feeling of horror. And the same goes for Ceauşescu's architecture. The blocks around the great boulevard are designed eclectically, combining all kinds of architectural styles. At first they look like replicas of the same kind of neo-classical houses that one finds in most European cities; but their ornamentation (balconies, arcades, arches, etc.) combines neo-gothic, neo-baroque, modernist and old Romanian architectural elements, which together create a post-modern effect. If the traditional socialist apartment block represents all that is ugly in architecture, Ceauşescu's buildings try to embody all that is supposedly beautiful.[21] However, it is precisely this excess of "beauty" that causes his architecture to look like kitsch.[22]

How does the present Romanian regime perceive the palace? In a brochure written for visitors, the palace is first described as "a 'giant' built during the 'golden age' of the dictatorial regime and born in the mind of a man for whom the nation of 'reasonable sizes' did not exist".[23] The palace is claimed as the second-largest building in the world (after the Pentagon), but the most prominent because it is the most disputed. This controversy almost resulted in its annihilation, but: "Realizing its enormous value, in fact a Romanian inheritance in danger to be destroyed and robbed, people began to look at the building with less hostility and named it the 'People's House'." The rest of the text reads like Ceauşescu's promotion material, with its descriptions of the glory of the palace and what the people sacrificed for its completion. Thus, we are reminded that this is "not a palace from Aladdin's stories, but a real one, showing the true wealth of Romania: stone, marble and wood from the Romanian mountains and forests . . . Today, the monumental building stands for the most precious symbol of democracy in Romania, that is the Parliament, serving the high and noble aim we have all aspired for: equal and complete representation of the Romanian people."

By presenting the palace as a national symbol, the current political elite has specifically incorporated this traumatic construction into its political discourse. The symbolic power of the building, supposedly made only from Romanian materials, is strengthened by the fact that it was produced through the enormous hardship of the Romanian people. However, it is essential to appreciate how the palace has realized Ceaușescu's original intention. As a parliament, the People's House is made to stand for the "complete representation of the Romanian people". This all-encompassing construction could be understood as the final stage of Ceaușescu's vision, which tried to give form to an ideal total society. Thus, when today's regime claims that it completely represents the people, Ceaușescu's dream of totality is, in some way, realized.

Ceaușescu is not the only megalomaniac who has tried to change reality to fit his ideal. Surprisingly, many past and present architects have tried to do the same, limited in their endeavor only by lack of power and resources. Even in contemporary American architectural inventions – the shopping malls and Disneyland – one can find points of comparison with Ceaușescu's project.

THE MALL OF ROMANIA

In today's world, we are witnessing the slow disappearance of the city, since the machinery of cyberspace has erased the cement of traditional urban planning, thus creating a new kind of city, "a city without a place attached to it".[24] However, there is yet another significant change in contemporary architecture – the construction of *a place without a city*. The prototypes of this type of construction are shopping malls and Disneyland. My claim is that Ceaușescu's project tried to realize the same utopia of building a place without a city and that such a vision is not far from what malls or Disneyland represent in America. Let us first point out the similarities between the idea of the mall and Ceaușescu's project.

It is essential to both projects that they erase the symbolic dimension of the city. Ceaușescu tried to do so by flattening the old part of Bucharest and by demolishing old villages. In a more subtle way, the malls are doing the same: they are destroying the social fabric of suburban towns by causing small shops to go out of business and by offering new, supposedly public spaces in their stead.[25] For the mall developers, it is essential that, on the one hand, the mall appears as the new public space in American suburbia, but on the other hand, that it is legally defined as a private place, which limits the rights of visitors to engage in activities that do not meet with the approval of the mall's management. In the mall, people are not allowed to hold demonstrations, distribute leaflets, sign petitions, etc., without the permission of the owners. Freedom of speech is, therefore, limited.

What Ceauşescu's project and the mall also have in common is surveillance. American malls are the panopticons of the twentieth century: hidden cameras view every corner, numerous guards observe people's movements, and the architecture itself (the way the mall is structured, where the entrances are placed, etc.) facilitates surveillance. In comparison to the mall, Ceauşescu's panopticon adopts a more traditional surveillance strategy. From the palace, which sits on an artificial hill (under which lie three floors of hidden tunnels), one has a view over a large part of the city. It is significant that the palace, observed from the avenue, appears to have no entrance; there are only numerous windows, which give the impression of an omnipresent gaze. The palace thus functions like the surveillance tower in Bentham's panopticon, where the observer remains hidden but his all-penetrating gaze is nonetheless always present.

What is the logic of this kind of surveillance? In the panopticon, to create the impression of the inspector's omnipresence, it is essential that he remain invisible, hidden in the tower, so that the prisoners never know when they are actually being observed. To obtain this effect, the inspector need not be actually present; it is enough that the prisoners assume his presence. The inspector need only occasionally expose a prisoner and reveal to him facts that show that he has been closely monitored; then the fear of being unknowingly observed will spread among the other inmates.[26] Surveillance under communism functioned in a similar way. The regime created the impression of omnipresence without controlling each individual; it was enough to strike only occasionally – randomly controlling a small number of people was enough to inspire fear among the population as a whole. Likewise, cameras in malls or theft-protection devices in shops also do not need to be operating all the time; it is enough to use them every so often and to publicly expose suspected thieves in order to create the impression of total surveillance.

Although Ceauşescu's project appears to be functionally very different from the mall, its economic purpose is actually the same. Both combine commercial and administrative spaces. American malls nowadays are no longer solely places to shop, but closed "cities" with offices, hotels, cinemas, entertainment centers, etc. Lacking the entertainment offerings, Ceauşescu's project nonetheless looks like an open mall: at the main crossroad of Avenue Uniri, one finds Bucharest's largest department store, while the whole avenue is lined with the small boutiques of world-famous designers, antique and jewelry shops, souvenir shops, etc. Plaza Uniri thus offers something for everyone: cheap department-store goods for the lower classes, souvenirs for the tourists and elegant clothing for the *nouveau riche*.[27]

Of course, one cannot claim that Ceauşescu's original idea was to build a socialist version of the shopping mall. However, both projects have the same goal of trying to realize a utopia. In 1900, the American writer Bradford Peck, who was also the owner of a department store, had already developed in his novel, *The World a Department Store*, an ideal social vision in which the state would resemble a department store that dutifully supplied its obedient citizens with all the goods they needed, from food to housing. Other well-known American utopias imagine a new world where the production process is reorganized so that people no longer need to work, but instead simply indulge their consumerist desires.[28] Such an American utopia is, of course, not so different from the communist one.

The ideology of the shopping mall is nicely supplemented with America's other great consumer-entertainment invention: Disneyland. As Margaret Crawford says: "While enclosed shopping malls suspended space, time, and weather, Disneyland went one step further and suspended reality. Any geographic, cultural, or mythic location . . . could be reconfigured as a setting for entertainment."[29] In Disneyland, national pavilions became "stand-ins for the act of travel itself, ersatz souvenirs. A trip to Disneyland substitutes for a trip to Norway or Japan."[30] But significantly, Disneyland does not try to reproduce reality in the same way that wax museums do: Disneyland, according to Umberto Eco, "presents its reconstructions as masterpieces of falsification".[31] It therefore produces a "reality" that is admittedly a fantasy. As Eco points out: "Disneyland not only produces illusion, but – in confessing it – stimulates desire for it: A real crocodile can be found in the zoo, . . . but Disneyland tells us that faked nature corresponds much more to our daydream demands."[32] Hence, technology is perceived as something that can produce more reality than nature itself.

What is repressed in this acknowledgment of fantasy is the reality of capital: Disneyland can easily admit to being a fake, but never openly acknowledge that all its fantasy houses lead to another shopping experience. But to gain the freedom to shop, the visitors freely submit themselves to the constraints of the place: surveillance by the guards, long waiting lines, impersonal voices over the loudspeakers telling them what and what not to do, etc. The Romanian Securitate would have been thrilled to have had such power over people. But my idea here is not to make a Foucauldian analysis of surveillance in contemporary society, pointing out how no significant differences exist between socialism and Western democracies; my concern is rather to ask: what is the logic of the fantasies produced in architectural settings like Ceauşescu's project or Disneyland, and for whom are these fantasies staged?

The similarity between Disneyland and Ceauşescu's project concerns primarily their designers' perception of reality and fantasy. Ceauşescu incorporated into his fantasy construction all the "best" architectural forms from Athens to Paris and Rome. Here again the fiction is more real than the reality itself.[33] One no longer needs to go to Paris or Rome to admire the real stuff, when Bucharest offers the best replicas of all these places. But there is one crucial feature specific only to Ceauşescu's project: for his fantasy project to attain the status of reality, the original, the "real" reality has to be destroyed or at least prohibited. Ceauşescu, of course, could not annihilate the boulevards of Paris, but he could forbid his people to visit them. While Disneyland convinces you in a "democratic" way that there is no point in going to see the original, since the faked thing is much more enjoyable, Ceauşescu has to prohibit the original.

This is also obvious from the way his second architectural project was conducted – the construction of a new type of socialist village. In the last decade of his rule, Ceauşescu decided to transform the countryside, eliminate the old villages and build model socialist rural centers. With his program of so-called systematization, Ceauşescu wanted to realize the ideal of a harmonious distribution of productive forces all over Romania. To achieve this goal, villages were supposed to be "transformed into industrial *agricultural or agro-industrial* towns . . ., becoming polyfunctional communities with all the economic, socio-demographic, urban and cultural features of socialist civilization". [34] This project caused enormous suffering for those people who were displaced from their old homes and forced to live in the new soulless "villages", which were composed of poorly constructed apartment blocks, sometimes without running water.

Today Bucharest has a "Ceauşesculand", officially called the Museum of Romanian Villages, where one finds a compound of actual remnants of the old Romanian rural village houses and, of course, souvenir shops. If, with Disneyland, one does not need to go to Japan anymore, because the pavilion of ersatz "Japan" replaces the real thing, in "Ceauşesculand" one can enjoy the old villages, but the real thing has been destroyed.

For whom is an architectural fantasy like Ceauşescu's project or Disneyland staged? The answer is for the big Other, or better, for that point in the social symbolic structure known as the Ego Ideal – with which the subject identifies and from where the subject sees him or herself in the way he or she wants to be seen. In the previous chapters, I have analyzed how the subject identifies with his or her Ego Ideal in love relationships, but to explain the logic of the subject's identification with the Ego Ideal in the social domain, let me take another architectural example. In the early twenties, Le Corbusier wanted to build an ideal city. His idea was to tear down part of Paris and build a new center composed of skyscrapers with skywalks and gardens underneath. This new city would provide the environment that Le Corbusier saw as "inherent in an advanced industrial society".[35] For Le Corbusier, his project was thus a fulfillment of the demands of some greater order – the principles of industrial society. These principles were for Le Corbusier the big Other for whom his fantasy was staged; or, more precisely, he had posited this principle in place of his Ego Ideal, from where he then observed himself in the way he wanted to be seen – as a dutiful creator who would make reality accord with the Ideal. Similarly, for Disney the big Other was the world of technology realized most perfectly in the movies. Disney's "cartoon utopia"[36] was just the first stage in reproducing the perfect world of technology, since he intended to build an actual city that would represent the proper urbanism of the electronic age. Disney died before realizing this dream, but his successors have recently completed the project. In Florida, they built a highly secured city called Celebrations, where people's lives are totally controlled and their social space is structured in the way Disney envisioned. Ceauşescu also succeeded in realizing his utopian city. For him, the big Other was the ideal communist society. He simply perceived himself as the executor of this higher will: it was the ideal of the future classless society that demanded changes in urbanism. Ceauşescu identified with the point in the social symbolic structure from which he then saw himself as the creator who would refashion reality to correspond to the ideal. His love for Romania was thus primarily love for the communist ideal, which led him to mutilate the existing face of his country.[37]

The difference between the two projects reflects the contrast between socialism and capitalism. Under socialism, a belief in reality still existed – which is why Ceauşescu had to actually tear down the city. Under capitalism, however, one does not need to destroy an existing reality in order to achieve a desired goal, i.e. the owners of new shopping malls have no need to demolish the old village's shops, since these businesses will sooner or later close down on their own. Capitalism can thus build new fantasy places and the virtual reality of the capital will, in its search for higher profit, slowly cause the destruction of old public spaces and small owner-businesses.

Under socialism, ordinary people, like prisoners serving life terms, believed that pure freedom could exist without the big Other. But when the big Other of communist ideology collapsed, they either sought in vain for new ideologies and new institutions that would grant them stability, or they cultivated memories of the "happy" past. In the end, people with a nostalgic need for the big Other are not so different from their fallen leader. Both organized their identities around the communist ideal. The difference is only that Ceauşescu believed in the big Other's existence and presented himself as a tool in its hands, while the people did not believe in the big Other, even though their entire identity was wrapped up in it. The paradox of the big Other is that it does not exist, but nonetheless functions. And the tragedy of the Romanian story is that Ceauşescu did not realize that the big Other is just a symbolic fiction, while at the same time, the people did not recognize that this fiction had more power over them than they ever imagined.

NOTES

1. New political elites exploit this nostalgia by creating populist ideologies that promise to re-establish the security of the good old days without communist totalitarianism. For example, General Alexandr I. Lebed, who was a rising star in Russian politics in the mid-nineties, liked to appeal to the disenchanted masses by promising them the end of corruption and the establishment of order, claiming that "life under the new democratic regime is far worse than in Soviet times. 'There was stability,' he [Lebed] said. 'A 120-ruble pension was enough for a more or less decent life. You could study for free. You could get free medical assistance, not the best but

decent. You could get a cheap holiday. Eighty percent of the population relied on these natural privileges' " (*New York Times*, October 13, 1995).

2. The paradox is that these people mostly do not come from the ranks of the previous Party establishment (since many of the latter quickly became new capitalists), but from the working classes. In the past, they had often been privately critical of the regime and made jokes about it, but publicly they meekly obeyed the communist rituals.

3. Stephen King, "Rita Hayworth and Shawshank Redemption", in *Different Seasons*, New York: Penguin 1982, p. 105.

4. Ibid., p. 49.

5. Ibid., p. 97.

6. Red tastes this "freedom" when Andy tells him about his plan to establish a hotel and encourages him to join him in business: " 'You think it over,' he [Andy] said casually . . . And he strolled off, as if he were a free man who had just made another free man a proposition. And for a while just that was enough to make me *feel* free. Andy could do that. He could make me forget for a time that we were both lifers, at the mercy of a hard-ass parole board" (ibid., p. 79).

7. Ibid., p. 96.

8. Ibid., p. 99.

9. This feeling of guilt is further elaborated in Chapter 3 of Renata Salecl, *The Spoils of Freedom: Psychoanalysis and Feminism after the Fall of Socialism*, London: Routledge 1994.

10. Sigmund Freud, "Screen Memories", *Standard Edition*, vol. III, p. 307.

11. Jacques Lacan, *The Four Fundamental Concepts of Psycho-Analysis*, trans. Alan Sheridan, New York: Norton 1977, p. 49.

12. Ibid., p. 50; translation modified.

13. Among the demolished buildings were 26 churches and 2 monasteries. Some 40,000 inhabitants were displaced from their homes.

14. During their many friendly visits to North Korea, Ceauşescu and his architects quickly noted Kim Il Sung's architectural inventions and then realized them in Bucharest, making them even more flash. See Gheorghe Leahu, *Bucurestiul disparut*, Bucharest: Editura Arta Grafica 1995, s. 119. See also Pierre v. Meiss, "Fragmentiertes Bukarest", *Werk, Bauen + Wohnen* 3 (1993), as well as Catherine Durandin and Despina Tomescu, *La Roumanie de Ceauşescu*, Paris: Editions Guy Epaud 1988.

15. The earthquake that struck Bucharest in 1977 greatly "helped" Ceauşescu, since some of the buildings were destroyed. It is rumored that Ceauşescu was so afraid of death, he ordered studies to establish which part of the city was less likely to be struck by a future earthquake. He then built his palace there.

16. Today, attitudes to the Palace are paradoxical, with disgust mixed with secret admiration. Along with the new ruling elite, the Gypsies – the most

victimized group – are also enchanted by the "beauty" of the Palace. Rich Gypsies, for example, ask the architects who design their houses to use architectural elements from the Palace. The Gypsies were not supporters of Ceauşescu, since his regime treated them in the most racist way. Their admiration for his architecture, therefore, reveals a strange identification with their persecutor.

17. Jacques Lacan, *The Ethics of Psychoanalysis*, trans. Dennis Porter, London: Routledge 1992, p. 212.
18. Ibid., p. 211.
19. Jacques Lacan, *Seminar II: The Ego in Freud's Theory and in the Technique of Psychoanalysis*, trans. Sylvana Tomaselli, New York: Norton, 1989, p. 185.
20. Ceauşescu was obviously interested in regulating water, since in the early eighties he also built a Danube–Black Sea canal, again spending enormous sums of money. But when the canal was opened, "the volume of shipping traffic passing along it was only 10 per cent of that previously predicted. Domestic traffic even had to be re-routed to make the waterway appear busy." See Martyn Rady, *Romania in Turmoil: A Contemporary History*, London: IB Tauris 1992, p. 66.
21. It is well known that in architecture a building becomes a public place when it retains a "lack" that can be filled by people's fantasies, while "perfect" architecture, like Ceauşescu's, desperately tries to erase this "lack".
22. The Palace, a mixture of architectural styles, looks like a combination of a castle and Moscow's university Lomonosov. Added to this design are Greek columns and Roman arches. But the real excess is the inner decoration: the marble, wooden decorations, kitsch neo-baroque furniture and carpets. Significantly, the most luxurious room, which was constructed for meetings of the Party's Central Committee, is now called the "Human Rights Room".
23. The leaflet for visitors to the palace, entitled "International Conference Center", Bucharest: Artmedia Group.
24. Michael Sorkin (ed.), *Variations on the Theme Park: The New American City and the End of Public Space*, New York: Hill and Wang 1992, p. XII.
25. One finds another type of alternation between private and public in Orange County, where homes are

> technically "privately owned", because their ownership is in the hands of individuals, not corporations, [but] freedoms traditionally associated with private ownership no longer exist. One finds, for example, restrictive rules binding home owners vis-à-vis such matters as the species of shrubberies which can be planted in the yard, the types of dogs they can own, as well as the . . . color restrictions on house exteriors . . . The rules constraining home owners in Irvine read much like those which occupants of military housing

must sign before moving in, and for good reason" (Dean MacCannell, *Empty Meeting Grounds: The Tourist Papers*, New York: Routledge 1992, pp. 82–3).

26. See Jeremy Bentham, *The Panoptical Writings*, ed. Miran Božovič, London: Verso 1995. Miran Božovič points out in his introduction that Bentham's inspector has the attributes of a God-like being, a being whose power comes from a fictional presupposition of its existence. Here the fiction of the God has more power than any real God could have, since the omnipresence of God relies precisely on his ability to observe us without ever being observed himself. Lacan pointed out that people love God precisely for the fact that he does not exist. This notion has to be read together with Lacan's claim that love aims at the lack in the other; thus we love in a person what is more than he or she in him- or herself—the point of impossibility in the other. In regard to God, this lack in the other concerns the very non-existence of God, the fact that he is a nonentity.

27. Paradoxically, today's "realization" of Ceauşescu's project is a new mall that was built on the outskirts of Bucharest, where one can find the best hotel in the city, a congress center and a mall of luxurious shops. Today this hermetically closed place is a haven for upper-class Romanians, but with its tight security and luxurious goods, it also presents the ideal of a post-Ceauşescu era.

28. Edward Bellamy, *Looking Backward*, New York: Penguin Books 1960. See also Margaret Crawford, "The World in a Shopping Mall", in Sorkin (ed.), *Variations on the Theme Park*, p. 19.

29. Crawford, "The World is a Shopping Mall", p. 16.

30. Michael Sorkin, "See You in Disneyland", in Sorkin (ed.), *Variations on the Theme Park*, p. 216.

31. Umberto Eco, *Travels in Hyperreality*, New York: Harcourt Brace 1990, p. 43.

32. Ibid., p. 44.

33. In this search for beautiful architecture, Ceauşescu's project resembles the American architectural movement of the end of the nineteenth and the beginning of the twentieth centuries – the so-called city beautiful project. At that time, American architects built wide avenues and city squares resembling those of European cities. The idea behind this architectural movement was that one needs to embellish the city, introduce some order in its planning and clean it up, in order to change public life for the better, By changing the structure of the city, the planners hoped to introduce more humanity into people's lives and encourage them to develop a new interest in the idea of beauty and the arts. See M. Christine Boyer, *Dreaming the Rational City: The Myth of American City Planning*, Cambridge, Mass.: MIT Press 1986.

34. Ion Iordacel, "Dynamic of Social Structure in the Present Stage of Devel-

opment in Romania", in John W. Cole (ed.), *Economy, Society and Culture in Contemporary Romania*, Research Report Number 24, Dept. of Anthropology, University of Massachusetts, Amherst 1984, pp. 19, 20. Iordacel explains Ceauşescu's program of systematization: "Through a rigorous, scientific analysis of socio-economic, political, and cultural realities, comrade Nicolae Ceauşescu, in a valuable, creative and original synthesis, has shown a deep understanding of the qualitative and quantitative transformations in our country, the dynamic of Romanian society in the future . . ." when, as Ceauşescu predicted, "our socialist society will reach a superior level of civilization, the material and spiritual level of the people will increase, and the human personality will multilaterally flourish" (Report on achieving the decisions of the XIth Congress of the Romanian Communist Party, 1978, ibid., p. 16).

35. Robert Fishman, "Utopia in Three Dimensions", in Peter Alexander and Roger Gill (eds.), *Utopias*, La Salle, Quebec: Open Court 1984, p. 104.
36. Sorkin (ed.), *Variations on the Theme Park*, p. 232.
37. The film *Boxing Helena* (Jennifer Chambers Lynch, 1993) deals with similar mutilations in a love relationship. A young doctor obsessed with a beautiful and unattainable woman mutilates her by cutting her arms and legs. Thus he literally puts his ideal (immovable) love-object on a pedestal.

5

LOVE ME, LOVE MY DOG: PSYCHOANALYSIS AND THE ANIMAL/HUMAN DIVIDE

OF DOGS AND MEN

Why is the dog such an attractive animal for human beings? From Antiquity, there is the well-known case of the philosopher Diogenes who found in dog life the ultimate model for human life and himself decided to live like a dog. He thus wore few clothes, lived in a barrel and liked to masturbate in public, all to show his contempt for civilization and admiration for nature. With his rude behavior, Diogenes liked to provoke his fellow men, in order to prove that they were too weak to compete with him. For example, he boasted that no one dared to go hunting with such a distinguished dog as he.

Recently, the Western art world got a new, dog-like human being in the persona of the Russian artist Oleg Kulik. He usually has a dog-house built for a performance, and lives in the gallery day and night totally naked, walking and barking like a dog (Figure 8). He became famous when he started biting visitors to two art shows in Zürich and in Stockholm. In both cases, the organizers of the shows called the police, who enchained Kulik and took him to the police station for questioning. At first, the shocked policemen did not believe that Kulik had been invited to the exhibition to act like a dog. But, when the organizers of the show confirmed the story, Kulik was released, since it was unclear what he could be accused of.[1]

Before dealing with the problem of what it means to behave like a dog, let me note that I personally do not see great artistry in Kulik's biting viewers of his performance. The Kulik affair, however, can help us to address some theoretical issues that concern the divide between human beings and animals, which is for Jacques Derrida the last metaphysical divide not yet deconstructed.[2] But let us see, first, how Kulik's case undermined the naive belief in the idea of artistic dialog, and, second, how it restated the whole problem of the East–West relationship.

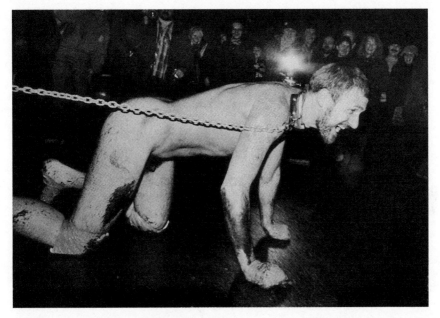

Figure 8 Oleg Kulik as a dog. (Courtesy of the artist.)

The *Interpol* exhibition in Stockholm was presented as an attempt to establish a dialog and a new form of communication between artists from the East and artists from the West. If one does not restrict one's understanding of communication to the Habermasian ideal-speech situation, where the parties involved tolerantly exchange ideas, thus creating an ideal democratic universe, but also follows contemporary psychoanalytic and post-structuralist reasoning, then communication becomes much less ideal. We know from the theory of Foucault as well as from Deleuze and Guattari, that communication, dialog and the exchange of ideas are all means of engaging in various forms of power struggle. And as Chapter 6 shows, debates about violence of language, the so-called hate-speech, have clearly proven that a simple speech act can contain the most aggressive racist attack. On the one hand, dialog and communication can involve a great deal of violence. But, on the other hand, someone can understand violence and destruction as a way to communicate. Thus, if the organizers of *Interpol* want to have dialog as the form of the exhibition, they should not be too surprised if some artists use violence and destruction as a mode of communication.

The paradox of the second problem is that Kulik was invited as a peculiarity – as a Russian dog. I am certain that if an American artist played a dog, he would be of much less interest on the international art scene than a Russian artist. We all know that the majority of people in today's Russia live a dog's life. And the first association with Kulik's performance is that he represents this reality of contemporary Russia. Kulik the dog thus interests the Western art world because he is a Russian "dog".

The trauma of the West in regard to Russia in recent years is that the West regards Russia as a superpower, but only on condition that it does not act as one. And, in regard to Kulik's performance, the West finds aesthetic pleasure in observing the Russian "dog", but only on condition that he does not behave in a truly dog-like manner. When Kulik ceased to be a decorative art-object – the Eastern neighbor who represents the misery of the Russian dog-like life – and started to act in a way that surprised his admirers, he was quickly designated the enemy. His performance (together with the performance of another Russian artist, Alexander Brener, who at the Interpol show destroyed a work by the Chinese-American artist Wenda Gu) was described as a "direct attack against art, democracy and the freedom of expression" and as a "classical model of imperialist behavior".[3] Here we encounter a deadlock similar to the way multiculturalists tend to treat the other. The other has to be a passive, submissive victim-like other; and if the other fails to be so, he or she is quickly designated as imperialistic, fundamentalist, totalitarian, etc. (Remember how the Bosnians, once they ceased to play the role of victims and started to arm themselves, were quickly named Islamic fundamentalists.[4])

The paradox of Kulik's performance is that his aim is not to expose his peculiarity as a Russian artist, but to answer the universal questions of the man–animal relationship, man's place in nature, etc. In the catalogue of the 1996 *Manifesta* show in Rotterdam, where Kulik played Pavlov's dog, we are given some answers in the form of the program of Kulik's art, written by his collaborator Mila Bredikhina.

The program closely resembles the theory of so-called "deep ecology" and its criticism of anthropocentrism. Kulik thus propagates a new agro-cultural revolution, which would bring a new symbiosis between humans and animals; he wants to limit human population to a third of its present

LOVE ME, LOVE MY DOG

size to establish a new balance in the biosphere; but in particular, he wants to encourage studies of the psychology of animals, which would result in a new dialog between animals and human beings. In this program, we also read that man should stop perceiving animals as the non-anthropomorphical Other, and begin seeing them as his alter ego. However, this only becomes possible if we question the entire logic of the organization of human society and especially the nature of democracy. For Kulik: "True democracy can only be established on the politically inclusive idea of zoocentrism (man is but a part, rather than a measure of our planet's biosphere). Zoocentrism integrates man as a subculture in the larger whole of a united culture of the noosphere (derived from *noos*: the ability to smell, to feel)."[5] Since ideal democracy is not possible, one should recognize that actual democracy resembles a jungle, where some inhabitants take advantage of the fact that they are stronger or faster than others. Thus Kulik concludes: "A jungle is in fact a more efficient society, devoid of the oversophistication that is currently stifling humanity. The main thing is that the jungle is the only place where the strong, the wise, and energetic can bring all their capabilities into play." However, Kulik's program also demands some improvements for the "democratic law of the jungle", such as "the further escalation of political inclusiveness, legal foundations of bioethics, universal suffrage, etc.".[6]

The theoretical position of deep ecology is much more radical than traditional ecology or environmentalism.[7] In its demand for the protection of nature, the latter still takes the human being as the center of the world. It claims that nature has to be protected because it presents a vital environment for humans. Deep ecology opposes such a view; from its perspective, we need to totally give up on anthropocentrism to create a new form of society relying on a symbiosis of nature and human beings.

Deep ecology has many troubling theoretical positions, but for the purpose of my argument I will invoke only two – the problem of the Cartesian subject and rights. Deep ecology finds the main culprit for the lack of the symbiosis between humans and animals in the notion of the Cartesian subject. Critics usually focus on Descartes's perception of animals as soul-less machines and on his devalorization of nature. But deep ecologists are wrong to regard the Cartesian subject as the ultimate anthropocentric notion: it was actually the advent of Cartesianism and the Copernican revolution it entailed that deprived the subject of its rooting in nature as well as its central place in the universe. On the one hand, the subject became pure substanceless subjectivity with no determined place in nature or culture, but, on the other hand, the subject also became one among many elements of the universe.

The modern notion of rights was established on the basis of this subject. Although in the contemporary understanding of rights, nature and especially animals receive more and more legal protection, it is clear that the human subject is still perceived as the dominant bearer of rights. In their fight for equal rights for humans and animals, the deep ecologists rely on utilitarian theory and its claim that each being wants to maximize its happiness and avoid suffering. As Peter Singer says: "it is not in my interests to suffer. If I am suffering, I must be in a state that, insofar as its *intrinsic* properties are concerned, I would rather not be in."[8] For deep ecologists, animals are similar to human beings in this avoidance of suffering, which is why they should be treated in the same way as humans.[9]

If psychoanalysis teaches us anything, it is that human beings are not inclined to achieve happiness. On the contrary, they find special enjoyment in suffering. And the whole history of psychoanalysis is concerned with discovering the mechanisms that drive the subject on this path of self-destruction. The ecologists' insistence on the avoidance of suffering may be true for animals, who could be said to be driven by the instinct of self-preservation; however, for humans, it is the opposite – as beings of language, they are essentially marked by a force of self-annihilation, i.e. the death drive.

Precisely because the human being is no longer a natural being, he or she has lost the ability to instinctively avoid suffering; however, to say it with Kant: by ceasing to be a natural being, the human being has acquired a freedom that allows him or her to feel sympathy with the suffering others – with animals, for example – and develop responsibility toward them. Thus: "We have seen men sacrifice their lives to protect whales; . . . [while] the reverse is far less common."[10] It can also be said that a man biting an animal is treated as responsible for his behavior and may be punished for his violent act, while in the reverse case one cannot speak of responsibility. Here Kulik's claim that he is a dog who bites also raises the question of responsibility.

When Kulik was taken to the police station in Stockholm, at some point he stopped playing the dog and started to give reasons for his act. He put some blame for his behavior on the visitors who treated him as a dog by teasing him, kicking him in the head, etc. Kulik also complained that the organizers had put him on too long a chain, which allowed him to go outside the bounds of the warning sign "Dangerous dog!" It was crucial for Kulik-the-person not to take responsibility for the behavior of his other self, Kulik-the-dog. However, at the police station, he also did not want to be treated like a dog – without the right to explain his action.

In medieval Europe, animals were treated as responsible for their wrong-doings. There are well-known cases of weevils put on trial for invading a vineyard, leeches prosecuted for their invasion of a lake, and so on.[11] In court, animals were represented by a counsel chosen for them, who usually defended their action by claiming that, as creatures of God, animals have the same rights to live in a certain environment or to consume plants. In many trials the animals won the case, and as a result the municipality had to give them compensation in the form of land where they could live freely without intruding upon the lives of humans. As might be expected, the insects weren't too pleased with such a decision and rarely moved to the designated place.

Deep ecology objects to the laws that protect animals and nature because they treat the latter only as the property of humans. And the new equalization of the rights of animals and humans that deep ecology insists upon would change the status of animals as property; animals would not be protected in the interest of humans but in their own interest and for their own inherent value.[12] One has the impression that before the emergence of capitalist society and its notion of property, animals were better treated by the law. But the paradox here is that the very idea of animal protection emerged only when the law started to regard them as property.[13] Thus it is only in the early nineteenth century that anti-cruelty statutes became an essential part of Anglo-American law. This legislation applied first to domestic animals like cattle, and it took some time before pets, like dogs and cats, were perceived as property, too, and thus acquired legal protection. Since the dog is regarded as property, this also implies the responsibility of the owner: it is the owner who is prosecuted if his or her dog bites people.

I assume that Kulik would support the deep ecologists' claim that animals should not be treated as property: however, in practice, Kulik acts differently. Whenever Kulik is invited to a show, he insists that he cannot travel alone, but needs to be accompanied by his owner – his wife. Now, let's speculate that Kulik was tried for his offense in court, and that the judge took him to be a dog and not a human being who is merely playing a dog.

Since the law no longer allows animals to be tried, the only way for it to deal with Kulik's offense would be to try his owner – his wife.

PAVLOV WITH FREUD

As for Kulik's attempt to create a new "united culture of the noosphere", which would be based on the ability to smell, or to feel – one can only respond that culture as such (in contrast to nature) was established at the moment when human beings ceased to rely on their sense of smell.

Jacques Lacan points out that what prevents the dog from rising to the level of man is its strong sense of smell.[14] Through the sense of smell, the dog still has a direct relation to objects, while with man this ability has been lost. Here we can take into account Freud's thesis that a crucial step in the history of humanity was when man stood up and stopped orienting himself primarily by smell, but rather with the help of his eyes. From that moment, excrement also was perceived as something that smells bad and as something by which one is disgusted.[15] Freud points out in particular that young children feel no disgust toward excrement; on the contrary, excrement is perceived as part of the body. It is only socialization that introduces disgust toward excrement: the child's anal eroticism has to undergo the phase of "organic repression" when the child is being formed into a social being.

Freud also says that "man scarcely finds the smell of *his own* excreta repulsive, but only that of other people's. Thus a person who is not clean – who does not hide his excreta – is offending other people; he is showing no consideration for them."[16] We perceive such behavior as an abuse and sometimes we say that such a dirty person is behaving like a dog. However, Freud concludes that: "It would be incomprehensible . . . that man should use the name of his most faithful friend in the animal world – the dog – as a term of abuse if that creature had not incurred his contempt through two characteristics: that it is an animal whose dominant sense is that of smell and one which has no horror of excrement, and that it is not ashamed of its sexual function."[17]

In contrast to the animal, the human being, by gaining his erect posture, has not only lost his ability to smell, but also the ability to copulate in an animal way. As is well known from the history of psychoanalysis, in the process of becoming a speaking subject the human being undergoes symbolic castration which introduces a bar, a lack, forever depriving the subject of the wholeness that animals still have. This also prevents the subject from finding sexual satisfaction in simple copulation. As Freud points out, with erect posture, it is not only anal eroticism that falls victim to organic repression, but the whole of the subject's sexuality.

The animal therefore still has the wholeness, as well as the ability to obtain sexual satisfaction, that the subject lost upon entrance into language. Animals and humans thus differ essentially because of language. Lacan deals with this difference in his seminar on identification, where he argues that it is not only the subject who lives in language but also domestic animals; but their relationship toward language is different. To illustrate this point, Lacan takes the case of his own dog Justine, named after the Marquis de Sade's novel. Observing how this dog behaves toward her owner, Lacan, he shows that the dog speaks, communicates with him, and shows her love and affection, and even jealousy. The dog is thus in language. But for Lacan it is crucial to point out that the dog has a very different approach to language from man's. The dog speaks only when she needs to speak, because of some inner pressure, or need. Only then does the dog establish a relationship toward the other, but this other is not the big Other in the sense of the social symbolic order. So the dog is in language, but she does not relate to the chain of signifiers – the big Other.

Let us illustrate this point by reflecting on Pavlov's famous experiment.[18] Pavlov tried to show that a repetition of some act – feeding the dog at the sound of a whistle – at some moment produces the effect that the mere sound of a whistle, unaccompanied by food, incites the dog to produce saliva, which otherwise happens only in reaction to food. The animal thus develops a conditional reflex, which is no longer linked to some real stimulus (food), but to a purely symbolic one (the whistle). Lacan's thesis is that Pavlov actually behaved as a structuralist *avant la lettre*, since his experiment confirms the function of the signifier and does not, as Pavlov mistakenly thought, simply give evidence about the functioning of the dog's brain. In Pavlov's view, the experiment was supposed to prove that with dogs the conditioned reflex always exists, while Lacan points out that such a conclusion is purely ideological, since it masks the fact that it is only the signifier that incites this reflex.

Lacan further maintains that the subject of Pavlov's experiment is not the dog, but actually Pavlov himself. The dog has no interest in the whistle, but only in the meat. The experiment was not intended to introduce any change: to amend or to impair the condition of the dog. As such, the experiment was of interest only to the experimenter Pavlov. It can even be said that the experiment proved the existence of none other than Pavlov, or as Lacan says, "there is no other subject here [in this experiment] than the subject of the experimenter".[19] What does this mean? The whistle has a meaning only for Pavlov: it is the signifier that represents the subject of science (Pavlov) for another signifier – the production of saliva. The subject of the experiment was thus Pavlov the whole time: he was the agency of the experiment, and he was also the one who gained satisfaction out of the knowledge that the experiment was supposed to establish.

Doesn't Kulik's *Manifesta* performance also simply demonstrate the existence of the experimenter? The paradox of Kulik is that he pretends to be Pavlov's dog, while in actuality his role is none other than Pavlov's. Kulik thus wants to be a dog, but actually ends up representing Pavlov, since here it is also Kulik himself who is the subject of the experiment. But this time he is the scientist who no longer needs the dog to validate his theories – the best results are gained when the scientist becomes the dog himself. In the final instance, Kulik's performance proves Lacan's point that the dog does not care about Pavlov's experiment – so why deal with the real dog? The trouble with Kulik is that he tries to look and behave as much as possible like a real dog, and does not recognize that it is only a human being who can enjoy this game – that is why no dogs come running to his show.

If Kulik's experiment cannot prove anything except his own existence as experimenter, what is his enjoyment in the show, and also, why is the public attracted to his performance? Continuing this line of thought, what is the enjoyment of the dog which the artist tries to imitate?

For domestic animals it is crucial that they live in language, since we cannot say that a dog, for example, behaves in the same way when it lives in nature as when it lives in a house. Language introduces change in the dog; in the case of Pavlov's dog, it can even be said that language makes the dog neurotic. However, this neurosis is in no way similar to the hysterization of the human being, which, as previous chapters show, is essentially linked to the subject's questions about the desire of the Other. In Pavlov's experiment the dog does not become troubled with the desire of the experimenter. Dogs do not question the desire of the Other. And this is what distinguishes them from human beings. However, this lack of any question about the desire of the Other is also what makes dogs more lovable than humans.

Why does this happen? Why are we so much in love with our pets that we even act in disregard of their well-being – for example, by dressing up dogs and cats? One possible explanation of this love is that humans see in animals some lost freedom, wildness, animality, etc., that they themselves no longer have. The animal would thus stand for the natural object, which is forever lost for the human being and which he or she still nostalgically mourns. Another explanation is that the animal presents for the human being an ideal other. It can even be said that the dog became man's best friend because man cannot be man's best friend.

The fact that a domestic animal lives in language means that it has been trained, pacified in a way that suits humans. Nonetheless, the animal is not barred by language and is thus not marked by a constitutive lack; thus the animal is not submitted to the logic of desire. The lack that marks the speaking subject forever prevents the subject from finding satisfaction, from fulfilling his or her desire – the subject is thus endlessly perturbed by his or her own desire and with the desire of the Other.

EATING NOTHINGNESS

In Kafka's story "A Fasting Showman", the main character gets immense pleasure from public fasting; his only complaint is that he is not allowed to fast longer than forty days. When at some point people become bored with his fasting performances, the circus is the only place remaining where he can still perform, but even there he gets little attention. Completely forgotten by the public, he is finally able to fast as long as he wants. One day, the circus overseer decides to use the fasting showman's presumably empty cage for some better purpose; but while cleaning the cage, he discovers that the fasting showman is still half-alive under the dirty straw. With his last strength, he reveals his secret, saying that he shouldn't have been admired for his fasting, since fasting was something he simply had to do. Or, better, he could not do anything else but fast. When the overseer asks why not, the fasting showman responds, "speaking . . . right into the overseer's ear, so that no syllable might be lost, 'because I couldn't find any food I liked. If I had found any, believe me, I should have made no bones about it and stuffed myself like you or anyone else' ".[20]

With this revelation, the fasting showman gives us the perfect definition of the logic of desire. The subject who is marked by an essential lack never finds the object that would fill this lack: as in the fasting showman's case, there is no proper object (food, for example) to satisfy the subject. One way for the subject to deal with this problem is to go endlessly from one object to another, while always remaining unsatisfied. The second option for the subject is to give up the search for the proper object and find *jouissance* precisely in this very abstinence – for example, in fasting.

One example of such a restraint is anorexia. Psychoanalysis understands anorexia as a form of hysteria, bound up with the subject's problem of desire. This impasse of the subject's desire is essentially linked to the problem of the mother's desire. Lacan points out that usually the anorexic was nurtured with too much love as a child, even to the point of being fed too much. In this case, the child's refusal of food paradoxically can be understood as the way the subject deals with his or her own desire in regard to the mother's love. The mother's love blocked the child's desire, so for the child rejecting this love through the refusal of food is the only way to keep his or her desire in motion.

Psychoanalysis links anorexia with the hysteric's demand that her desire remain unsatisfied. This dissatisfaction is connected to the subject's failure to find the object that would fill the lack; thus in the final instance there is no way to escape the bar that marked the subject when she entered language. In the case of the anorexic, however, the subject has a very peculiar way of dealing with this lack. The anorexic is thus not someone who does not eat, but someone who eats precisely this "nothing" – the lack itself. Similarly, the fasting showman fasts because he did not find the food that would satisfy his desire. The deadlock of his desire brings him to the point of self-destruction; until his very death he eats "nothing" in order to keep his desire unsatisfied.

It is crucial for both, the fasting showman and the anorexic, that they need the big Other who observes their doings and whom they try to convince that they can go even further in their sacrifice. This need for recognition is what is essential for the hysteric. In Kafka's story, the fasting showman wants to be recognized by the Other even when he is dying; thus he tells his story in the overseer's ear so that nothing will be lost.

At the end of Kafka's story, we learn that the circus authority later put a young panther in the fasting showman's cage. In contrast to the fasting showman, the panther has no problem with his desire. Thus one would not expect the panther to find enjoyment in fasting because the panther "lacks nothing", not even freedom: "his noble body, furnished almost to bursting point with all that it needed, seemed to carry freedom around with it too; somewhere in his jaws it seemed to lurk; and the joy of life streamed with such ardent passion from his throat that for the onlookers it was not easy to stand the shock of it. But they braced themselves crowded round the cage, and did not want ever to move away."[21] In the case of the panther, language has introduced no lack; this gives him a mark of self-sufficiency, which makes him at the same time attractive and horrifying.

Kulik also tries to obtain this animal wholeness and self-sufficiency by playing a dog. Kulik tries to realize in the flesh the deep ecologists' desire to return to the state of nature. He thus hopes to rediscover in his dog-like body the lost object of desire, in order to attain a wholeness that man lacks. However, Kulik cannot escape the burden of being a human subject. This is clearly proven by his desperate need for the audience, the gallery or, in general, the big Other. Kulik, like his predecessor Diogenes, finds enjoyment in posing as a dog only when others observe him. It may be harder for humans to learn self-sufficiency from dogs than for dogs to learn language.

A man who behaves like a dog hopes to escape the big Other and find true enjoyment, the lost animality of human nature. However, here we can invoke Lacan's famous reversal of Dostoevsky's phrase "If God doesn't exist, then everything is permitted", into "If God doesn't exist, then nothing at all is permitted any longer".[22] Thus the man who rejects the restraints of human rituals and behaves like a dog will not find the desired satisfaction, but even more prohibitions. For Lacan, only a saint in his asceticism might find *jouissance* that is not linked to the big Other. But there are no gallery openings for a saint's performance.

NOTES

1. Kulik's imprisonment in Stockholm was a paradoxical event, since the organizers of the art show knew beforehand about his troubles with the police at the show in Zürich. However, they thought that was just part of the game. But when Kulik started biting visitors in Stockholm, the organizers were so shocked that they called the police themselves.
2. See Jacques Derrida, " 'Eating Well', or the Calculation of the Subject: An

Interview with Jacques Derrida", in Eduardo Cadava, Peter Connor and Jean-Luc Nancy (eds.), *Who Comes After the Subject?*, New York: Routledge 1991.

3. See "An Open Letter to the Art World", *Siksi* 1 (1996).

4. For an analysis of the Western media's representation of the victims of the Bosnian war, see Renata Salecl, *The Spoils of Freedom: Psychoanalysis and Feminism after the Fall of Socialism*, London: Routledge 1996.

5. See the catalogue of *Manifesta 1* biennial exhibition, Rotterdam 1996.

6. Ibid. "This law is to become political reality when all the biological species of the planet enjoy equal political rights. The first steps on this road have already been made: the Political Laboratory of the Biosphere and the Party of the Animals (Kulik's Party) have been successfully functioning in Russia for two years" (ibid.).

7. See George Sessions (ed.), *Deep Ecology for the 21st Century: Readings on the Philosophy and Practice of the New Environmentalism*, Boston: Shambala 1995.

8. Peter Singer, "The Significance of Animal Suffering", in *Behavior and Brain Sciences* 13 (1990), p. 11.

9. Daniel C. Dennet points out the distinction between pain and suffering in animals and humans. He agrees with the ecologists' position that animals feel pain, but not with the claim that the notion of suffering applies to animals in the same way as to humans: "Snakes (or parts of snakes!) may feel pain ... but the evidence mounts that snakes lack the sort of over-arching, long-term organization that leaves room for significant suffering" (Daniel C. Dennet, "Animal Consciousness: What Matters and Why", *Social Research* 3 [1995], p. 707).

10. Luc Ferry, *The New Ecological Order*, Chicago: University of Chicago Press 1995, p. 41.

11. Ibid. See also Jean Vartier, *Les Procès d'animaux du Moyen Age à nos jours*, Paris: Hachette 1970.

12. For a detailed analysis of the ecologists' objection to the treatment of animals as property, see Gary L. Francione, *Animals, Property, and the Law*, Philadelphia: Temple University Press 1995. See also Tom Regan, *The Case For Animal Rights*, Los Angeles: University of California Press 1983.

13. See Jerrold Tannenbaum, "Animals and the Law: Cruelty, Property, Rights ... Or How the Law Makes up in Common Sense What It May Lack in Metaphysics", *Social Research* 3 (1995).

14. See Jacques Lacan, *Identification*, unpublished seminar (1961–62).

15. Later studies in biology complicated this hypothesis, since they showed that for higher primates, like chimpanzees, vision is also much more important than the sense of smell. Similarly one finds with these primates, as well as with cats and birds, a tendency to get rid of their excreta and to "teach" their offspring to do so.

16. Sigmund Freud, "Civilization and its discontents", *The Penguin Freud Library*, vol. 12, Harmondsworth, Middx: Penguin 1985, pp. 288–9, footnote 1.
17. Ibid.
18. See Jacques Lacan, *The Four Fundamental Concepts of Psycho-Analysis*, trans. Alan Sheridan, New York: Norton 1977; as well as the unpublished seminars *L'Angoisse* (1962–63) and *L'acte psychanalytique* (1967–68).
19. Lacan, *The Four Fundamental Concepts of Psycho-Analysis*, p. 228.
20. Franz Kafka, "A Fasting Showman", in *Wedding Preparations in the Country and Other Stories*, Harmondsworth, Middx: Penguin 1978, pp. 173–4. This short story is also known as "A Hunger Artist".
21. Ibid., p. 174.
22. Jacques Lacan, *The Seminar II: The Ego in Freud's Theory and in the Techniques of Psychoanalysis (1954/5)*, trans. Sylvana Tomaselli, New York: Norton 1991, p. 128.

6

SEE NO EVIL, SPEAK NO EVIL: HATE SPEECH AND HUMAN RIGHTS

What is going on when someone utters "hate speech"? What does a speaker hope to accomplish by disparaging members of another nation or race, by proclaiming the Jews guilty of all kinds of conspiracies, by declaring homosexuals social misfits or by publicly denouncing women as inferior human beings? Would someone who publicly blames blacks, Jews or even single mothers for all the troubles of society actually be happier if these people were simply to disappear? Of course not. It is common knowledge, for example, that one encounters a higher incidence of anti-Semitism in countries where there are very few Jews, such as in the Austrian provinces before the Second World War. If the goal of hate speech is not really to change anything, then what is its intention? And how can we control its effects?

Lacan's theory suggests an understanding of the problem of violence and speech that differs from that of structuralist and post-structuralist theories primarily because he does not give way on the issue of responsibility. Additionally, psychoanalysis can help us to reassess the dilemma currently posed by cultural relativism, which arises from the fact that every culture has a different understanding of violence and every culture also has a different understanding of those universals – human rights, equality, freedom – that motivate its attempts to combat violence. The problem with cultural relativists is that they do not see that their tolerance of difference is always only a different form of tolerance, which allows their governments to deal with ethnic and racial conflicts in other nations according to their own interests.

THE VIOLENCE OF WORDS

Is the subject whose speech hurts a member of an ethnic minority or race responsible for his or her action? Relying on deconstructionist theory, Judith Butler has offered one way to answer this question: the subject who utters injurious speech merely quotes from the existing corpus of racist speech; he or she repeats, re-cites, fragments of the discursive environment, of the reasoning and habits of the community. The subject who is perceived as the author of injurious speech is therefore only the effect, the *result*, of the citation, and the fact that the subject appears to be the *author* of the utterance simply disguises this fact.

For deconstructionists, the relevant question is thus: who should be punished for injurious words? Shouldn't history itself be put on trial instead of an individual subject? The subject, as the fictitious author of the words, has been burdened with responsibility so that this history can be masked. Since history itself cannot be put on trial or punished, the subject becomes its scapegoat. If those who utter injurious speech merely cite from some pre-existing social and linguistic context, and by so doing become a part of the historic community of speakers, society is wrong to impose responsibility for injurious speech on a single subject.[1]

One is tempted to say that in this approach to injurious speech there is no place for individual responsibility. But in fact the deconstructionist position is not so straightforward, for increasingly it is maintained along-side an insistence on "political correctness". That is an insistence that language must be changed so that it no longer reflects racial, sexual or ethnic prejudice. One would not be wrong to summarize this insistence on "political correctness" as the demand that the subject feel guilty and that he or she vigilantly and constantly question his or her identity and motivations. The most popular critical position these days steers an odd and unsuccessful course, maintaining, on the one hand, that the context totally determines the subject, and, on the other hand, that the subject must distance him- or herself from this context by constantly apologizing for uttering improper words. The shortcomings and inconsistencies of this position lead us to seek fresh inspiration in psychoanalysis.

THE BIG OTHER AND THE PAIN OF THE VICTIM

Before addressing the problem of responsibility as it is raised in psycho-analysis, let me first explore the matter of the intention of the subject who verbally attacks a member of a religious minority, another race, and so on. It can be argued that the subject who utters a racist slur seeks a response, and that there are two possible types of response. As those American critical-race theorists who favour "hate speech" legislation correctly point out, the prime intention of injurious speech is to provoke the person assaulted to question his or her identity and to perceive him- or herself as inferior.[2] But the speaker also seeks another response: by uttering injurious speech the speaker searches for confirmation of his or her own identity. Attempting to overcome an uncertainty in this regard the speaker engages in race-bashing in order to define him- or herself as part of the racist community that would grant him or her stability.

In hate speech, one encounters the same logic that is found in all forms of violence, which is always aimed at ruining the fantasy scenario that sustains the identity of the person being harmed or even tortured.[3] The target of violence is the unsymbolizable kernel in the other: the object a – the object cause of desire. It is around this object that the subject forms its fantasy, its scenario of provisional wholeness. In hate speech, we are dealing with the attacker's demand that the victim question this perception of wholeness, his or her sense of identity. Since one's identity has its roots in the object a, the slandered person or race cannot offer a defense through recourse to the "truth" or to a critique of the ideology that underpins the slanderer's attack. Hate speech is so insidious because it is designed to take advantage of the victim's structural "defenselessness".

But the goal of injurious speech is not simply to humiliate the other, to assign a subordinate place to the person being verbally attacked; it also seeks to assign a special place to the one who speaks. Here Althusser's theory of ideological hailing comes in handy.[4] When a policeman hails an individual on the street, his intention is not only to assign a subordinate place to the addressee (to interpellate him as an ideological subject, as Althusser points out), but also to define his own position in regard to the addressee. Through the act of hailing, the policeman demonstrates that he has authority and can force the person he hails to accept this fact. The violence of the performative is thus defined not only by what it does to the addressee, how it assigns him or her a place in the social symbolic structure, but also by the way it forces the addressee to recognize the speaker's authority. By uttering a performative statement, the speaker primarily expresses a desire for recognition. So, when I as a subject am hurt and humiliated by someone's demeaning remark, I assign, through my very injury, authority to my accuser.

We must, however, be precise about the authority that the sender of the injurious message wants the addressee to sanction. Where does this image of authority emanate from? Here one again encounters the Lacanian big Other, the social symbolic structure, since it is from the big Other that the subject receives his or her symbolic identity. The subject constantly searches for the point in the symbolic universe from which he or she will appear likeable to him- or herself, and in racism this symbolic identification plays a major role. The social symbolic structure within which racism is at work is always already in place, otherwise the racist speaker would have no independent idea that words have the potential to wound. One can thus agree with deconstructionist critics that the subject always quotes from the vast historical corpus of racist vocabulary and that it is never the individual subject who invents racist speech. But with every racist sentence, one must add, the subject reinstalls this symbolic space anew. For the existence of the big Other is radically dependent on the subject.

By uttering racist speech, the subject seeks out the Other that would confirm his or her identity and grant his or her authority. And paradoxically, it is the addressee of this speech who plays the role of the "mediator" between the sender and the big Other: by recognizing him- or herself as the addressee of the sender's words, he or she actually occupies the place in the symbolic structure from which the speaker receives confirmation of his or her identity and authority.

This demand for recognition of authority is not only part of assertive speech but also determines the logic of speaking in general. Every act of speaking involves this demand for recognition from the big Other: every sentence that the subject pronounces constructs a big Other that has to hear it and grant the subject his or her identity, i.e. affirm him or her as a speaking being.[5] But while every speaking being in some fundamental way constructs the big Other and simultaneously charges it with recognizing him or her, the racist goes a step further by making him- or herself an *instrument* of the Other, the "values of Western civilization", for example.[6] When the racist attacks blacks, he or she does so as the Other's "mouthpiece", as it were; he or she speaks on behalf of the Other, who is really speaking through him or her. The racist can thus be certain about him- or herself only on two conditions: that the big Other exists, and that he or she is the Other's tool. By what means does the racist acquire confirmation that these conditions are met? Paradoxically, confirmation comes from the reaction of the victim.

As I mentioned earlier, the racist targets in the victim the traumatic kernel around which the victim organizes his or her identity. Words can only injure if and when the victim is so struck by them that he or she cannot immediately reflect upon them, when he or she is either totally mute or is only able to respond with violence. In sum, the most horrible verbal violence happens when the victim cannot respond rationally, when words hit the very kernel of the victim's being. The famous 1942 case *Chaplinsky v. New Hampshire*,[7] which introduced the notion of "fighting words", presents an almost Lacanian reading of this phrase. The court ruled that "fighting words" are not protected by the First Amendment because they have a direct tendency to cause acts of violence by the person to whom such words are addressed. The court also explicitly stated that words count as fighting words when they are "said without a disarming smile".[8]

When his injurious words hurt the victim so much that the only possible response is violence, when his or her speech touches the traumatic object in the victim, the racist receives proof of the Other's existence. The pain of the victim constitutes the ontological proof of the existence of the Other for the racist. When the victim is so hurt that he or she cannot respond, the racist needs to convince him- or herself that the injury was justified. The paradox is that the racist first needs some (racist) theory that allows him or her to perceive the verbal assault against the victim not as injurious malice but as a justifiable act, and yet it is the victim's pain which provides the very validation he or she seeks. In sum: for the racist, the Other always has to be firmly in its place so that the racist can sustain his or her perverse fantasy of serving the Other's *jouissance*.

This fantasy is also sustained through the formation of a community.[9] Not only does the community vindicate the racist's fears, the fears themselves vindicate the excessive commitment to the community. A simple belief in the danger of foreigners is insufficient to sustain the dread that constitutes racism; what is necessary is the knowledge that others perceive the same danger. In other words, it is not so much one's own private belief as one's belief in the belief of others that "justifies" for the racist the violent

SEE NO EVIL, SPEAK NO EVIL   123

hatred he maintains toward all who are foreign. At the same time, however, it is the foreigner or victim of racism who is the condition for the possibility of one's belief in and commitment to one's racist community. The invention of the dangerous Other (blacks, Jews, and so on) acts as a kernel of the master signifier to unite the disparate elements and problems of a complex society and to give them a clear and coherent meaning. This enemy Other lends consistency to the community in which we dwell by becoming the easily grasped cause of all its ills. It is easy to see, then, that the type of victim "in vogue" at any given moment goes hand in hand with the ideological definition one gives to one's society. In the mid-nineties, a poll taken by the *New York Times* revealed that the majority of Americans who lost their jobs blamed not the boss or the owner of their company, but the Democratic government, which they felt was running the country so badly that their bosses had no alternative but to lay off workers. While in the late nineties, when the political Right came into power, new culprits were found in single mothers and their "criminal" children.

This circular relation between the community and its Other raises the question of *jouissance* and thus of responsibility. If a community's victim can be said to be its symptom, it then becomes evident that the community holds itself together by means of a vital attachment to an intense negative pleasure – or *jouissance*. Psychoanalysis has always held the subject responsible for his or her *jouissance*, beginning with Freud, who spoke of one's *choice* of neurosis. Consider, for example, the case of Dora. While it remains true that she lived in problematic family and social circumstances – her father was unprincipled, Herr K. was a lecherous family friend, his wife had strange sexual tastes, and her own mother was strangely absent – psychoanalysis forces us to observe that none of the "objective" circumstances explains Dora's investment in the whole affair. The question remains: what did she get out of being the victim of these circumstances; what type of *jouissance* bound her to this unpleasant group of characters? Analysis would be forever blocked if this question was never posed, and the situation would be simply incomprehensible.

Recognizing this responsibility for one's *jouissance* distinguishes Lacanian theory from structuralism and also from deconstructionism. Clearly we can agree that the subject is determined by a social symbolic structure, and that in hate speech the subject cites from the vast history of racism. Nonetheless, the subject "chooses" to speak. Although the words may escape the subject's intentions, and he or she says more in slips of the tongue or between the lines, the subject cannot escape responsibility, even if this responsibility accounts for no more than the mere fact that he or she is a subject.

THE REMAINDER

We cannot, of course, determine what is at stake in the use of hate speech without clarifying its relation to language in general. Psychoanalysis is founded on the fact that something in language escapes our grasp. Some incalculable element is always at work in language, which emerges unexpectedly and undermines what we are trying to say. Lacan called this element llanguage (*lalangue*), and Jean-Jacques Lecercle[10] called it the remainder. The remainder is that something in language that exceeds not only the speaker's control, but scientific inquiry as well.

The science of linguistics is endlessly concerned with delineating llanguage, with giving language a coherent form through a series of universalizing propositions, so that it will, in the final instance, be thought to be able to say everything. Referring to Lacan's *L'Etourdit*, Jean-Claude Milner has shown that for this possibility to be established, something must be left out of language: "in order for any All to be said, a limit is needed which, in suspending it, would guarantee it as an All constructible in a predetermined way."[11] The limit that totalizes language and encourages our belief that we can "say it all" is what excludes llanguage – the remainder, the leftover that insists in language:

> Llanguage is made of a bit of everything, of what wallows itself in the gin-mills, and of what we hear in the salons. On each side, we encounter the misunderstanding, since, with a little of good will, it is possible to find a meaning in everything, at least an imaginary one. Did he say "dide" or "Dieu"? Is this "croate" or "cravate"? . . . The llanguage is the storage, the collection of traces which other "subjects" have left, i.e. that, with the help of which, let's say, each subject inscribed its desire into llanguage, since the speaking being has to have a signifier to be able to desire; and desire in what? in its fantasies, i.e. again in signifiers.[12]

Language inscribes itself as a whole by prohibiting something, by ruling something out of bounds. Take as an example of llanguage a child's babbling of improper words and sentences: one cannot say that these prattling forms do not issue from language. Yet it is precisely because these incorrect forms are, in a certain respect, part of language, made up of it, that they have to be dismissed from it. The domain in which language and llanguage confront each other, the domain where prohibition takes place, is *speech*. It is when the words are spoken that the prohibition of llanguage is set in motion. Thus, the insistence of linguistics on the delineation of correct and incorrect forms is determined by the fact that, as Lacan points out, "saying is of the order of not-all – 'all cannot be said' ".[13] To retain the image of its universality, the science of linguistics has to insist on a limit; it has to determine what "cannot be said" by a given language.

Llanguage is thus simultaneously part of language and outside it, prohibited. For Lacan, language is both the result of the exclusion of llanguage and also the source of its construction. Language is thus a scientific concept invented by a master, or, better, language is a scientific way of dealing with llanguage, a way of understanding it. As Jacques-Alain Miller says: "language is the effect of the discourse of the master, its structure is the very structure of the master's discourse."[14] The master imposes himself onto llanguage, captures and articulates it in order to form the body of language so that language becomes something that can be written. This mastery of llanguage is the task of all the theories of language (grammar, phonetics, logics, etc.) "by means of which the speaking being paves its way through llanguage, conceptualizes it, even if only by alphabetizing it".[15]

Lacan's main point is that the aim of llanguage is not communication and he thus makes the unconscious his prime example of llanguage. Communication implies reference, which the unconscious lacks; this is made clear by the fact that the effects of the unconscious disrupt the whole body, as well as the soul.[16] The unconscious bears witness to a knowledge that escapes the speaking being. Accordingly, Lacan has described the unconscious as

> knowledge, a knowing how to do things (*savoir faire*) with llanguage. And what we know how to do with llanguage goes well beyond what we can account for under the heading of language. Llanguage affects us first of all by everything it brings with it by way of effects that are affects. If we can say that the unconscious is structured like a language, it is in the sense that the effects of the llanguage, already there qua knowledge, go well beyond anything the being who speaks is capable of enunciating.[17]

The subject can thus be said to understand jokes, slips of the tongue, and so on, not because of language but because of llanguage.

Through the remainder what is spoken is not only something more than an individual speaker's intention, but something more than the sum of the speech acts of the members of a linguistic community: "Even if someone invents the words, by the time they become a slogan they have lost their subjective character."[18] As pointed out by many contemporary theorists, including Deleuze and Guattari, the purpose of language is not simply to inform, communicate or solicit information, but to establish relations of power.[19] Language not only represents the world, but acts in it. In determining just how it acts, what it effects, we must not neglect to consider the struggle between language and its remainder. For if the latter can be defined as *"the return within language of the contradictions and struggles that make up the social, . . . the persistence within language of past contradictions and struggles, and the anticipation of new ones"*,[20] then it is not enough to say that, through the remainder, history speaks in the form of citation. Instead we must say that in the remainder it is the *antagonism* of this very history, the social symbolic struggle, that is inscribed.

Nor should we neglect the role of the remainder, of llanguage, in the functioning of hate speech. The subject understands hate speech as injurious not because he or she knows the meaning of the words uttered, or the structure of the language in which they are uttered, but because there is a remainder in language that disrupts this structure, and allows new meanings to be attributed to the words. Llanguage, as both lack and excess, is at the same time the point where the system fails, becomes uncertain, and the point where this lack is cancelled to become a surplus: "The map of [llanguage] is the map of the 'points of poetry' where lack is cancelled, where it becomes excess, and where what is impossible to utter is said in a poem."[21]

Hate speech could be perceived as another form of this excess, as a violent "poetry" that temporarily fills the lack in the symbolic structure. Hate speech simultaneously includes a certain social antagonism and attempts to annihilate it – though, of course, it constantly fails at the latter. This is why hate speech is not simply a form of citation, a repetition of some received idea or historical prejudice, but a "novel" way of stating some social antagonism.

Let's take the example of the racist attack at Stanford University in which two white students hung a poster of Beethoven repainted as a black man on the door of a black student. What is the message of this act? One might answer, "There has never been a black equivalent of Beethoven." But if one takes into account the current debates about affirmative action programs in universities, the poster also implies another meaning: "You have no place here, since, as a black man, you'll never be a genius." What is inscribed in this racist attack is thus not only a historical prejudice, but a bitter response to what the white students saw as a limitation on their own freedom and power.

THE VIOLENCE OF CULTURAL DIFFERENCES

Since each subject forms a different fantasy of his or her own integrity, that is, since every fantasy is specific to the subject who is structured by it, he or she also perceives differently the sort of violence that is capable of shattering such fantasies of wholeness. Similarly, different cultures understand violence in radically different ways. As Chapter 7 shows, certain initiation rites, like clitoridectomy, which appear to be essential in some non-European countries, strike Western eyes as forms of torture or mutilation. Such differences raise important questions about universal values such as human rights, freedom and equality, which are often invoked against perceived forms of violence. The question is: should these universal values, inventions of a West European tradition, be applied universally or only to Western nations? What happens when a non-European nation claims to live by different values and challenges the imposition of these others? In short: how should we react when a culture, in the name of its own traditional values and its own understanding of human rights, engages in practices that other cultures perceive as harmful?

In recent years, this dilemma has been exacerbated by various events: in the former Yugoslavia, Serbs have persistently claimed that what outside observers perceive as aggression against others is only their way of defending the human rights of their fellow Serbs, who are being tortured by neighboring nations; during the famous Rushdie affair, Muslims insisted that they must be free to resort to physical threats to protect the integrity of their religion. These transparent attempts to legitimize violence through a "re-reading" of certain universal values have to be considered alongside some current critiques of "Eurocentrism", which call for an end to all universals in the name of a wide-sweeping particularism.

We are now witnessing the emergence of a cultural relativism that forbids any intrusion into other cultures and confines the notions and application of universal values to Western civilization. These relativists seem to reason as follows: "We admit that our culture was imperialist in the past, but we now reject this past and embrace cultural differences; we therefore urge that our so-called 'universal' values not be imposed on others." True consistency in defending cultural relativism would require us to claim that we are not in a position to judge or actively oppose totalitarian regimes (fascism, Stalinism, Islamic fundamentalism, and so on), since they all emerged in historically different circumstances incompatible with our own.[22] Cultural relativists are forced to take the position: "We disagree, but we cannot contest others whose culture is so different from our own." This position is now often taken by Western governments faced with violent conflicts all round the world, from Bosnia through Rwanda to the forgotten case of East Timor, to mention only the most brutal cases. When dealing with countries like Cuba or Iraq, however, cultural relativists often become universal defenders of human rights and easily forget the Cubans' or Iraqis' right to determine their own values.

An example of this sort of cultural relativism is evident in the film *Before the Rain*, by Milcho Manchevski. Moving between London and a village in Macedonia where Orthodox Macedonians and Muslim Albanians engage in violent nationalist clashes, the film offers a "reflection" on the national struggles in former Yugoslavia. In the first episode, entitled "Words", a young Orthodox monk finds in his cell a frightened Albanian girl hiding from Macedonian nationalists who claim that she is a murderer. Once they track her down, the cycle of clashes that permanently shatters this peaceful region begins. The second part, "Faces", introduces Anne, a picture editor in London, and her lover Aleks, the charismatic Macedonian war photographer, winner of the Pulitzer Prize, who, after sixteen years of living in exile, decides to return to his village in Macedonia. Anne's dinner with her estranged husband in a chic London restaurant is interrupted by a loud argument between a waiter and a customer, both former Yugoslavs. The argument ends in a shootout that kills Anne's husband. The third episode, "Pictures", takes place when Aleks returns to Macedonia, where all the senseless violence alluded to in the first two episodes emerges in a new context, this time that of the overt hatreds between Muslims and Albanians who had lived peacefully together for decades. Aleks's fond memories of home are bitterly shattered and at the end he dies by the gun of his own cousin.

The film is full of symbolism about the regression of peoples into old historical patterns of nationalism and religious fervour. A typical Macedonian or Albanian is thus dressed up in a mixture of his or her national costume and typical Western clothes (kitschy t-shirts, sneakers, and so forth), ornamented with religious symbols, and shown holding a cellular phone in one hand and a Kalashnikov in the other.

The story does not follow a chronological sequence of events, but disrupts a temporal logic by mixing elements of life in London with those in Macedonia. For example, when Aleks is still alive, Anne is shown looking at pictures that will be taken at the end of the story, when he is killed. The structure of the film is circular: at the end of the first episode, the Albanian girl (who, as we learn later, is a daughter of Aleks's old love Hana) is killed by her brother, but the last episode concludes when Aleks, trying to save the girl, is killed by his own cousin's gun. This disruption of temporal logic and circular structure underline the timelessness and irrationality of ethnic violence.

Aleks's perception of the national conflicts in his former home is presented as a distanced and distorted vision through a camera. To the village doctor, the war appears as an infectious virus that can potentially spread anywhere and strike anyone: people in Bosnia, Macedonia and even Britain. The film, in general, presents violence as simple irrationality, as some deep-seated instinct which suddenly erupts with terrible force. We thus see a beautiful countryside where people live in old picturesque houses and are obsessed with national myths and religion. The film shows no signs of the ugly architecture of the "real" Macedonia: crumbling socialist apartment blocks, ugly factories, polluted cities, villages composed of rickety shacks, and so on. Group identities are deliberately blurred so that it ultimately becomes unclear what idea or ideal drives people to kill: is it nationalism, religion or something else? The final point is that none of these notions are worth dying for.

The "viral" explanation of violence reveals ideology operating in its purest form. According to this view, society is a body infected by a virus carried by fanatic nationalists. Viruses are invisible, one cannot easily detect the carrier, and no remedies (antibiotics) can help the body combat them. An infected body heals itself by creating its own antitoxins; no outside intervention will do. Such an explanation of violence, of course, assigns no role to politics; nor is there any need to analyze the situation that produces the violence.

In *Before the Rain*, the only thing that crosses the divisions between the two national groups is love: Aleks still loves his former girlfriend, Hana, who is now a widow; however, national hatreds preclude the realization of their love. And young Macedonians and Albanians still fall in love, as happens with Hana's daughter, though in the end they may be punished with death. And, significantly, most people die at the hands of their own people.

The film's perception of nationalism seems to have gone down well in the West. Its underlying message – people from this beautiful region are incomprehensible to our Western mode of thinking; something in these people, their primordial passions and hatreds, escapes our grasp – seems to please even the most educated Western film-goers. The extra-diegetic audience, in other words, is no different from the diegetic one. And what do they do in the face of this violence? The media publish pictures of killings in Bosnia, the people in the London restaurant become innocent victims of the "savages" who settle their account on the wrong terrain; in general, all that the observers can presumably do is to be shocked by the unbridgeable difference that separates them from these people.

ARE THERE DIFFERENT UNIVERSALS?

The relation between universal human rights and the right to cultural difference is one of the greatest antinomies of our time. As Cornelius Castoriadis has pointed out, this question is related to the fact that "we [Westerners] at the same time, claim that we are one culture among others and that this culture is unique since it recognizes the alterity of the others (which wasn't the case before, and what other cultures do not acknowledge to us)"; but we have, in addition, invented values we claim as universal.[23] To show that this problem is not only a theoretical issue, but one that must be dealt with in everyday life, Castoriadis cites the following example: let's say that you have a colleague of African Muslim descent, whom you value highly, and you learn that this person wants his daughter to undergo ritual circumcision. What should you do? The dilemma is this: if you do not say or do anything, you are not helping to protect the girl's universal human right not to be submitted to mutilation. But if you say something and try to change the father's thinking on this matter, you are robbing him of his culture, and, by doing so, transgressing the principle that incompatibilities between cultures must be respected. Castoriadis concludes that in such a case Westerners cannot give up on the values they have invented and believe to be valid for all people, regardless of their cultural background.[24]

Another conflict between universalism and particularism in human rights stems from the fact that we are referring here not only to the rights of the individual, but also to collective, group rights. Liberals and communitarians both believe most conflicts can be resolved by prioritizing particular rights; for liberals, individual rights take priority, for communitarians, group rights do. Yet in neither case does the choice serve to prevent violent collisions between the two or outright abridgments of seemingly fundamental rights. Let us take the famous American case *Santa Clara Pueblo v. Martinez*.[25] This case deals with the tribal custom and law according to which the children of women who marry men outside the tribe lose their tribal status. This custom does not pertain to men: if they enter an exogamous relationship, their children retain their tribal status and thus rights on tribal property. The Pueblo tribe claimed that patrilinear descent was essential for the preservation of their cultural identity, while the woman bringing the suit, Julia Martinez, challenged this law, arguing that the identity of the tribe had not always been founded on patrilinear order and that traditions of kinship had changed throughout the history of the tribe. In this case, the group right of the tribe eventually prevailed over the individual right of one of its members.

Other such conflicts are legion: in the United States, the Amish community's refusal to send their children to public school; in France, the insistence of Muslim women on their right to wear headscarves in school; and of African-Muslim women on their right to female circumcision.

And how are we to decide between the competing claims of individual rights and group identity when one's group identity accounts for a substantial part of one's self-identity? In other words, since the two kinds of rights are not mutually exclusive, a choice of one often diminishes or harms the very thing that was chosen.

A liberal response to these dilemmas is to argue that one has the right to submit oneself to whatever ritual mutilation one likes as long as one has been properly informed of one's choices and been given information that will allow one to make them. This, of course, raises the issue of what constitutes "proper information", since there is no neutral space for knowledge. The very space we perceive to be a place for the distribution of knowledge about alternatives to existing practices (a school, for example) may be perceived by some groups as a place for the violent erasure of knowledge about themselves and their own identity (as is clearly shown by the Amish case). In short, many of these dilemmas have no definitive answer; they simply cannot be finally resolved. And yet to throw up our hands in despair, as though there were nothing to be done, is to miss the point that the very invention of the notion of rights opened up the possibility of these ongoing debates and made the various conflicts visible.

Moreover, the fact that the notion of universal values was a product of European culture does not mean that it should be interpreted by a historical, genealogical approach or that its validity can be limited to this culture. For the fact is this notion cannot be historicized. We cannot account for the existence of the idea of human rights by pointing out that it emerged at a specific time in European history. As Castoriadis wrote:

> Contemporary Europeans ("European" here is not a geographical expression, it is an expression of civilization) do not take account of the enormous historical improbability of their existence. In relation to the general history of humanity, this history, this tradition, philosophy itself, the struggle for democracy, equality, and freedom are as completely improbable as the existence of life on Earth is in relation to the existence of solar systems in the Universe.[26]

This is true in a general sense; that is, no matter how we try to find the source of society's institutions, in God or in various gods, in the laws of Nature or Reason or among its ancestors, this source remains a necessary "self-occultation of the self-institution of society".[27]

But there is another, more specific sense in which certain aspects of European culture cannot be historicized. The moment universals such as equality and human rights were established, they lost their foundation by transforming their own history. Again, Castoriadis reminds us:

> The exigency of equality is a creation of *our* history, this segment of history to which we belong. It is a historical fact, or better a *meta-fact* which is born in this history and which, starting from there, tends to transform history, including also the history of *other* peoples. It is absurd to want to found equality upon any particular accepted sense of the term since it is equality that founds us insomuch as we are Europeans.[28]

Searching for particular historical foundations of universals, and thus relativizing them, presents a danger of profound absolutism, since I as the observer posit myself in a presumably neutral position from which I can judge history as I please. By doing so, I take it for granted that everyone accepts the same rationality as I do. I already presuppose the equality of humans as reasonable beings, which is not an empirical fact but is a hypothesis of all rationalist discourses. In the history of philosophy, for example, the most totalitarian theories were not those that spoke about abstract principles but those that were searching for objective empirical facts: empiricists were usually the ones who had put themselves into the position of abstract neutrality from which they then judged the supposed objectivity.[29]

An essential attribute of democracy is "active forgetfulness": for democracy to be established on the grounds of the empty space of power, one has to disregard its contingent origin. Democracy usually is established through some violent act, and can easily come to an end with the help of non-violent, democratic mechanisms, through elections, for example. This active forgetfulness is also at work in law, where, as Walter Benjamin pointed out,[30] the violence through which the law emerged is forgotten once the law is established. And the same goes for universals: for human rights to have an effect, for example, we have to forget that at the time they were established they pertained only to white male Europeans. In our understanding of universals, traces of racism and male domination remain, but since universals are empty by themselves, we have to constantly engage in the struggle for their meaning and for their expansion, so that they do not exclude groups of people. Active forgetting in terms of universals only means that their exclusionist history does not diminish their inclusionary character in contemporary democracy. To exemplify this ahistoric nature of universals, a parallel can be drawn to objects of art. Let us take the writings of Shakespeare: they were produced in a specific historical context, but they are nonetheless universal in their value. The great work of art outlives its history, it detaches itself from the specific circumstances that accounted for its production and becomes an object of eternal value. The value of a great work of art is as indeterminate as the object a is for the subject: neither one has a value; nothing in either the art object or the object a determines its cost; but nonetheless, each one keeps our desire in motion. In Lacan's theory, it is also the real that is universal: the real also outlives the historical context and always returns as the excess, something that social symbolic structures cannot symbolize or contain within a historical narrative.

Returning to the problem of universals, such as human rights and freedom, it is essential, first, that they remain open projects which are not historically determined, and second, that they open up the possibility of questioning the very society they emerged from. Such universals emerged when the subject lost its rooting in tradition, when he or she became empty, substanceless subjectivity marked by an essential lack. As Ernesto Laclau notes: "The universal is part of my identity insofar as I am penetrated by a constitutive lack (insofar as my differential identity has failed in its process of construction)."[31]

Different cultures perceive universals differently, since universals are always incorporated in a specific way into the fantasmatic structure through which a society deals with its own inherent antagonism, its own impossibility as a coherent whole. As long as universals are something that emerge out of this impossibility, something that tries to fill the structural gap in the organization of society, they are always inscribed in a specific way in the symbolic organization of society.

So how can we understand the way another society perceives its universals? For Castoriadis, "what is different in another society and another epoch is its very 'rationality', for it is 'caught' each time in another imaginary world. This does not mean that it is inaccessible to us; but this access must pass by way of an attempt (certainly always problematical; but how could it be otherwise?) to restitute the imaginary significations of the society in question."[32] So what is at stake here is our willingness to put ourselves in the skin of another and try to understand the logic of his or her reasoning. With the help of Lacanian psychoanalysis, Castoriadis's use of imaginary creations to describe the structures through which other cultures reason should be supplemented with the concept of the fantasy, since the fantasy is something other than imaginary creation, something that touches the unsymbolizable real. And here the problem begins, since it is the very core of society that we are dealing with when we try to understand the real, the unsymbolizable kernel around which society structures itself. The problem is thus that another culture structures itself differently around some central impossibility. What makes cultures similar is that both are crossed by an antagonism; but the way they deal with this antagonism is different.[33]

Let me return to the problem of hate speech, which, as pointed out earlier, very much touches the real, the kernel that causes us pain when we are submitted to verbal violence. Contemporary societies perceive this issue in a radically different way. Most lawmakers would agree that it is an issue that has to be dealt with somehow, but the legislation, and what this legislation protects, vary so widely from country to country that international human-rights organizations cannot establish any general rules regulating hate speech. With the exception of the United States, the majority of other countries, especially the European states, have legislation in their penal code that deals with hate speech. However, this legislation has different intentions in different countries. For example, in France and Germany, "hate speech laws" focus on anti-Semitism and the denial of the Nazi Holocaust. In the past, in the communist countries in Eastern Europe, the defamation laws were mainly used to protect the Party elite from the criticism of the masses, and today such laws re-emerge in some post-communist countries (Romania, for example). However in other countries, such as Indonesia and India, "hate speech" prosecutions tend to involve those who criticize a dominant religious group.[34]

What actually regulates injurious speech in society is not so much existing laws but what Hegel named *Sittlichkeit*[35] – the system of mores, ethical life. *Sittlichkeit* is what holds a community together, it is what envelopes the national substance. But it is essential that this *Sittlichkeit* remains contingent in relation to the law: the law cannot encompass ethical life. Ethical life always eludes legal regulations, but at the same time it provides a basis for the understanding of the law, i.e. the submission to the law by the public. For *Sittlichkeit*, it is crucial that it "enjoins us to bring about what already is":[36] it concerns "the norms ... of a society ... sustained by our action, and yet already there".[37] It could also be said that *Sittlichkeit* functions as an Ego Ideal, the instance we identify with in the symbolic order, the point from which we appear likeable to ourselves and thereby obtain our symbolic identity. However, this instance is not the same as the law itself.

The status of this *Sittlichkeit* is different in the United States because of the lack of a unified national substance. The USA as a melting pot or a salad bowl, as it is lately called, with its mixture of nationalities forming the nation, has replaced the uniform national substance with the Constitution – the word of the Founding Fathers. The Constitution works in America as a unifying principle that has the same logic as the nation in European democracies. And the way to express love of country and respect for the Founding Fathers is not national identification or nationalism, but patriotism – devotion to the father. The Constitution, especially its First Amendment, thus replaces the national substance and becomes the thing around which American *Sittlichkeit* forms itself.[38]

To exemplify how different *Sittlichkeit* is in various countries, let us compare Sweden and the United States in their attitude toward violence and pornography on public TV. Sweden, which is perceived as one of the most liberal countries in terms of sex, has a very tolerant approach to pornography, but it also has very strict rules regulating violence on TV. Thus, a lot of American films are not allowed to be shown on Swedish TV, but one can freely see pornographic films. In America, things are exactly reversed: on publicly accessible TV there are lots of violent films and no pornography. This example shows us how contingent society's reaction to violence is, and that there are no general rules determining what society perceives as its *Sittlichkeit*.[39] For this reason, there are no clear answers on how to regulate hate speech: language, at the same time, can and cannot be controlled, and the results of its control cannot be foreseen. In the end, the subject him or herself is ethically responsible for the *jouissance* of his or her speech.[40]

What we are witnessing today is a constant struggle over who will define universals and also over who will define injurious speech. The fact that even totalitarian regimes must invoke human rights and freedom, if only to legitimize violence, is a proof of the power of universals. However, universals are essentially empty, which is why we have to engage in the struggle for their content. And this struggle must move toward expanding universals, not toward limiting them to only some cultures. This very expansion is the only way for universals to gain new, and it is hoped democratic, meaning.

NOTES

1. See Judith Butler, "Burning Acts: Injurious Speech", in *Deconstruction is / in America*, ed. Anselm Haverkamp, New York: New York University Press 1995. An exemplary case of the ambiguity in Butler's position: "If the utterance is to be prosecuted, where and when would that prosecution begin, and when would it end? Would this not be something like the effort to prosecute a history that, by its very temporality, cannot be called to trial? . . . This is not to say that subjects ought not be prosecuted for their

injurious speech; I think that there are probably occasions when they should. But what is precisely being prosecuted when the injurious word comes to trial and is it finally or fully prosecutable?" (ibid., p. 156).

2. See *Words that Wound: Critical Race Theory, Assaultive Speech and the First Amendment*, ed. Mari J. Matsuda, Charles R. Lawrence III, Richard Delgado and Kimberle Williams Crenshaw, Boulder, Col.: Westview Press 1993.

3. On ruining the fantasy in war, see Chapter 1 in Renata Salecl, *The Spoils of Freedom: Psychoanalysis and Feminism after the Fall of Socialism*, London: Routledge 1994. See also Elaine Scarry, *The Body in Pain*, Princeton: Princeton University Press 1989, for a different but insightful approach to the "unmaking" of the victim's word by the torturer.

4. See Louis Althusser, "Ideology and Ideological State Apparatuses", in Louis Althusser, *Lenin and Philosophy and Other Essays*, London: New Left Books 1971.

5. As Lacan says: "What I seek in speech is the response of the other. What constitutes me as subject is my question. In order to be recognized by the other, I utter what was only in view of what will be. In order to find him, I call him by a name that he must assume or refuse in order to reply to me." Jacques Lacan, *Ecrits: A Selection*, trans. Alan Sheridan, New York: Norton 1977, p. 86.

6. This is a strategy similar to that of Ceauşescu, who, as Chapter 4 shows, also took himself to be an instrument of the big Other.

7. *Chaplinsky v. New Hampshire*, 315 U.S. 568 (1942).

8. Ibid., 568, 573 (1942).

9. See Etienne Balibar, "Is there a 'Neo-Racism'?", in Etienne Balibar and Immanuel Wallerstein, *Race, Nation, Class: Ambiguous Identities*, London: Verso 1991.

10. See Jean-Jacques Lecercle, *The Violence of Language*, London: Routledge 1990.

11. Jean-Claude Milner, *For the Love of Language*, trans. A. Banfield, London: Macmillan 1990, p. 101.

12. Ibid., p. 129; translation modified.

13. Ibid., p. 106.

14. Jacques-Alain Miller, "Théorie de lalangue – (Rudiment)", *Ornicar?* 1 (1975), p. 30.

15. Ibid., p. 31.

16. See Jacques Lacan, *Television*, ed. Joan Copjec, trans. Denis Hollier, Rosalind Krauss and Annette Michelson, New York: Norton 1990.

17. Jacques Lacan, *On Feminine Sexuality, The Limits of Love and Knowledge (Book XX – Encore 1972–1973)*, trans. Bruce Fink, New York: Norton 1998, p. 139.

18. Lecercle, *The Violence of Language*, p. 44.

19. Gilles Deleuze and Félix Guattari, *A Thousand Plateaus: Capitalism and Schizophrenia*, trans. Brian Massumi, Minneapolis: University of Minnesota Press 1987.

20. Lecercle, *The Violence of Language*, p. 182. "If the remainder has one rule to impose on the speaker, it can be only a form of double bind: I order you to disobey" (p. 137).

21. Ibid., p. 40. "Language is material not because there is a physics of speech, but because words are always threatening to revert to screams, because they carry the violent affects of the speaker's body, can be inscribed on it, and generally mingle with it" (p. 105).

22. If one were a cultural relativist living under Hitler, one would be consistent to reason: "Hitler and his neighboring nations just have a long history of disputes; as horrible as their crimes might be, they are part of the culture of the nations in conflict."

23. See Cornelius Castoriadis, *Philosophy, Politics, Autonomy: Essays in Political Philosophy*, Oxford: Oxford University Press, 1991, pp. 37, 38.

24. Ibid.

25. *Santa Clara Pueblo v. Martinez*, 439 U.S. 49 (1978). I rely here on the unpublished paper by Marty Slaughter, "Preserving Cultural Communities: Group Rights and Multiculturalism in American and Canadian Context".

26. Castoriadis, *Philosophy, Politics, Autonomy*, p. 135.

27. Ibid., p. 133.

28. Ibid., p. 135.

29. Ibid.

30. See Walter Benjamin, "Critique of Violence", in *Illuminations*, New York: Shocken Books 1967.

31. Ernesto Laclau, "Universalism, Particularism, and the Question of Identity", *October* 61 (1994), p. 89. "The universal emerges out of the particular not as some principle underlying and explaining it, but as an incomplete horizon suturing a particular identity. The universal is the symptom of a missing fullness and the particular exists only in the contradictory movement of asserting a differential identity." (ibid.)

32. Castoriadis, *Philosophy, Politics, Autonomy*, p. 67.

33. See Slavoj Žižek, *The Abyss of Freedom*, Ann Arbor: University of Michigan Press, 1997.

34. See *A Human Rights Watch Policy Paper: "Hate Speech" and the Freedom of Expression*, March 1992. "Indonesia's criminal code provides for the imprisonment for up to five years of 'anyone who publicly and deliberately expresses a feeling or undertakes an act of enmity, abuse or insult toward a religion followed in Indonesia.' This statute was used to prosecute Arswendo Atmowiloto, editor of *Monitor*, a Christian-owned newspaper, for publishing the results of a poll of its readership in which the prophet Mohammed ranked 11th (just after Arswendo) among most-admired

leaders. Arswendo began a five-year prison sentence on April 8, 1991"
(p. 6).

35. See Hegel, *Political Writings*, trans. T.M. Knox, ed. Z.A. Pelczynski,
Oxford: Oxford University Press 1964.

36. Charles Taylor, *Hegel*, Cambridge: Cambridge University Press 1975,
p. 376.

37. Ibid., p. 382.

38. The Constitution is read differently by different political groups. It is not
only that political discourse very much determines what counts as free
speech and that this interpretation changes significantly over time, but the
meaning of the Constitution itself comes out of the hegemonic struggles
that go on in American society. Usually, leftists claim that one has to
explain the Constitution by taking into account the historical situation in
which it was drafted, and rightists insist on the literal meaning of the
Constitution. But in contemporary political struggles it sometimes happens
that the Left starts insisting on the letter of the Constitution, on the
grounds that one should stick to the word of the Founding Fathers without
too much contextualizing of the Constitution and searching for a historical
explanation of its meaning. And it is the Right that insists on analyzing the
context of the constitution, pointing out how the interpretation changes
with historical circumstances. In the mid-nineties, this happened in the
debates around Proposition 487 that, in California, limited the rights of
immigrants since they are not citizens of the United States. When some
leftist lawyers opposed this proposition, they claimed that the Founding
Fathers did not use the word "citizens" but only "the people of the United
States". Thus it could be said that limiting the rights of non-citizens is
unconstitutional, since it is the people that are the subjects in the
Constitution.

39. As Kenneth Lasson points out:

> Swedes are far more interrelated with (sometimes dependent upon) their
> government than Americans. They appear to have great trust in their
> democratic process and look to it for the protection of their civil liberties . . .
> Thus the Swedish laws prohibiting defamation of race are, to the people who
> live under them, innocuous, particularly when contrasted with the oppression
> exercised by Nazi Germany, which threatened all of Europe in the name of
> race superiority. History, as well as philosophy, shapes society's degree of
> toleration for laws.

See Kenneth Lasson, "Group Libel Versus Free Speech: When Big Brother
Should Butt In", *Duquesne Law Review* 23:1 (1991), p. 89. "It has been
suggested [by David Riesman] that libel is more important in America than
in other Western democracies because an individual's reputation is considered akin to a property interest. Similarly, the role of the group in the

American social process has been subordinated to the role of the individual" (p. 117).

40. On Lacan's theory of ethics, see Alenka Zupančič, *Ethics of the Real: Kant, Lacan*, London: Verso, forthcoming.

7

CUT IN THE BODY:
FROM CLITORIDECTOMY TO
BODY ART

How can one explain the fact that today in the same district of New York one finds youngsters who decorate their skin with body piercing, artists who use body mutilation as a form of art and African immigrants who practice clitoridectomy? The last are usually fully integrated into Western society – they work or go to school, they participate in public life, etc. – while also retaining old initiation rituals. However, body mutilations, like clitoridectomy, are not simply the repetition of pre-modern forms of initiation; rather, they should be understood as a way in which the contemporary subject deals with the deadlocks in so-called post-modern society.[1] And some practices of body art, as well as the fashion of body-piercing and tattooing, can also be seen as ways of dealing with these deadlocks.

In this chapter I will compare the practice of clitoridectomy with the turn to masochism in body art. I am not claiming that these forms of body transformation are the same. What makes them comparable is that they are two different answers to the same question: what is the place of the subject in contemporary society?

Before analyzing the connections between these two practices, one needs to compare the different ways in which the subject identifies with the symbolic order in pre-modern, modern and post-modern societies. My intention, however, is not to trace the genealogy of these forms of society, but to take them as three different types of the subject's relation to the so-called big Other, i.e. the symbolic structure. If today people are returning to body painting or even to old forms of initiation, they are not simply copying past cultural forms; they are reinterpreting these forms in a new way. But to understand this reinterpretation, one must first understand the original meaning of initiation rituals such as clitoridectomy.

INITIATION AND INDIVIDUALIZATION

The ritual of clitoridectomy in Third World countries is a topic that from time to time attracts the attention of the Western media and provokes almost universal condemnation.[2] There are usually two types of reaction to clitoridectomy: first, the defenders of universal human rights want it to be strictly prohibited; second, those who insist on the right to cultural difference argue that though Westerners might be appalled by certain rituals in non-Western cultures, they have no right to impose their standards on non-Westerners. Things get even more complicated when Westerners realize that the ritual of clitoridectomy is performed not only in Africa and Asia, but also among immigrants in the heart of New York, London or Paris. Here legal prohibition has no real effect, since clitoridectomy is never performed as a public act, but as a secret ritual. From a Western point of view, it is shocking that clitoridectomies are performed in democratic societies.[3] It is also surprising that the development of capitalism in Third World countries has not contributed to its extinction; on the contrary, in some countries this practice has become even more widespread in recent years.[4] How can we explain this fact?

Women from ethnic groups that practice clitoridectomy usually claim that it forms part of their ethnic identity and has been performed for generations; and that by continuing to practice the ritual they are essentially contributing to the survival of their community's traditions. When members of such ethnic groups migrate to the West, they insist on their right to preserve their identity by means of clitoridectomy. Women also claim that if they have not been initiated via clitoridectomy, they cannot get married; and mothers who submit their daughters to the ritual usually argue: "If it was good for me, it will also be good for my daughter."[5]

While Westerners fear that the habits of immigrant non-Westerners will shatter the Western way of life, the immigrants complain that the prohibition by Western states of certain initiation rituals endangers their ethnic identity. It is thus not only Westerners who see the danger of the erosion of their culture in others (i.e. the immigrant cultures); the latter also perceive themselves as endangered by the dominant Western cultures.[6]

Chapter 6 pointed out the problems of cultural relativism in regard to clitoridectomy. This initiation ritual opens up further dilemmas that go far beyond the decision as to whether one is against it or in favor of it. The question is: what role does clitoridectomy play in the formation of women's sexual identity and how essential is this ritual for transmission of sexual norms from generation to generation? Further questions are: how does sexual difference inscribe itself in pre-modern and in modern societies? And how is one to understand a return to the cut in the body in post-modern society, for example in the case of some forms of body art?

Let me first summarize the explanations given by the supporters of clitoridectomy as to why this ritual needs to be preserved.[7] Although different ethnic groups usually justify clitoridectomy with different mythologies, one can make some comparisons between them. A widespread belief is that clitoridectomy assures a woman of her fertility. Various mythologies regard the clitoris as something impure and dangerous for the future child.[8] The clitoris is thus taken as a rival to the man's phallus. In Ethiopia, for example, one finds the belief that the uncut clitoris grows to the size of a man's penis and thus prevents insemination. And the Bambara from Mali claim that a man who has intercourse with an uncircumcised woman might die, since the clitoris produces a poisonous liquid. They also believe that at the time of birth one finds both female and male traces in a child. The clitoris is the trace of the male in the female and the prepuce is the trace of the female in the male. In order to clearly define the child's sex, one thus needs to extinguish the trace of the opposite sex via male and female circumcision.

Other justifications for clitoridectomy stress the importance of group identity. A woman who is submitted to this ritual becomes the equal of other women in her ethnic group – she is thus accepted in her community. The circumcised woman feels "pride in being like everyone else, in being 'made clean', in having suffered without screaming".[9] For women, to be different, i.e. unexcised or non-infibulated, produces anxiety: she is ridiculed and despised by the others, and she will also be unable to marry within her community.

Some ethnic groups also claim that clitoridectomy protects women from their excessive sexuality. Thus it makes them faithful. Since excised women are supposed to be less sexually demanding, men can have many wives and keep them all satisfied. Others argue the opposite: the excised woman is supposed to be more inclined to have extramarital affairs, since she is always sexually unsatisfied. But, a very common position is that clitoridectomy helps to retain a woman's virginity, which is especially important in the communities that make virginity the absolute prerequisite of marriage and in which women's extramarital affairs are strongly condemned.

Some defenders of clitoridectomy also claim that this ritual needs to be understood as an esthetic practice: the infibulated woman's sexual organ is supposed to be much more attractive than the non-infibulated one. And the most beautiful organ is the one that, after the scar is healed, feels smooth like a palm.[10]

Why do women who are submitted to the torturous practice of clitoridectomy not rebel against it? Why do they calmly accept mutilation of their genitals? And why do they force their daughters to do the same? The problem is not simply that women live in patriarchal societies in which they have no power to express their disagreement with rituals. Many cultures that perform clitoridectomy are not classical patriarchies – in some cultures men are even perceived as quite powerless[11] and considerable authority is in the hands of older women, who are cherished as father-like figures and as guardians of tradition, which is why they are entrusted with the task of carrying out clitoridectomies. The dilemma of why women support the ritual thus primarily concerns the position the subject has in his or her culture, i.e. the way the subject is entangled in his or her community.

Max Horkheimer[12] pointed out how, with the advent of the Enlightenment type of patriarchal family, one discerns a process of individualization that does not exist in the pre-modern family. The modern subject is, of course, linked to his or her tradition, family, national community, but this tradition is no longer something that fully determines the subject and gives him or her stability and security. The modern subject is expelled from his or her community – this subject is an individual who has to find and reestablish his or her place in the community again and again. That modern society no longer stages the ritual of initiation means that the subject must "freely" choose his or her place in the community, although this choice always remains in some way a forced choice. As we know from psychoanalysis, the subject who does not "choose" his or her place in the community becomes a psychotic – a subject who has an external relationship to the community and is not barred by language.

This forced choice, however, also enables the subject to experience some actual freedom, for example, to reject the rituals of the community. Only when the subject is no longer perceived as someone who essentially contributes to the continuation of his or her tradition, and as someone who is completely rooted in his or her community, does the moment occur when the subject can distance him or herself from this community, for example, by criticizing its rituals. Western feminists justly take clitoridectomy to be a horribly torturous practice. However, one can arrive at such a position only after going through the process of individualization, i.e. only when the subject has already made a break with his or her own tradition.

When we say that in pre-modern society subjects are not individualized and are thus not able to distance themselves from tradition, this does not mean that when people support clitoridectomy today they are falling back into pre-modern family organizations. On the contrary, the return to old traditions needs to be understood as a way contemporary subjects deal with the deadlocks in a highly individualized society. Thus when people propagate old initiation rituals they are not simply being nostalgic about the past or unable to oppose their tradition (usually they are quite willing to give up many other old rituals and prohibitions), but are trying to find some stability in today's disintegrating social universe.

There are various ways in which subjects deal with individualization in contemporary society. Young punks, for example, seem to respond to individualization by taking it to extremes: they adopt an ultra-individualized stance and constantly search for new body decorations to create a unique image. They make an effort to dress differently from the dominant fashion trends, but also strongly identify with a peer group. The punk's response to individualization is thus finally the formation of another group ideology. Although this ideology encourages individuals to look different, it nonetheless quickly forms new fashion codes. In contrast, an African immigrant might respond to radical individualization by strongly identifying with his or her ethnic tradition. In this case, too, group identity, paradoxically, appears as a solution to the deadlocks in individualization. If individualization first occurred when the subjects made a break with their tradition, the deadlocks accompanying individualization incite either a return to tradition or a formation of some new group identity.

THE IMPOTENCE OF AUTHORITY

It is well known that both types of initiation – male circumcision and clitoridectomy – are ways in which pre-modern societies mark sexual difference. In these societies, biological sex is not enough to ensure their reproduction. It is the symbolic cut made by the law, i.e. by language, that facilitates the continuation of tradition. The pre-modern society imposes all kinds of prohibitions and rituals that make a social being out of the human being. But the symbolic cut in the body, the inscription of a subject's identity, occurs as something real. In the act of initiation, the subject receives a physical mark on his or her body, in most cases through circumcision, but in some cases also through painting the body or tattooing it.

Some explain the rituals of initiation by claiming that pre-modern societies are based in the logic of repetition, which means that they do not question the nature and origin of laws, but only dutifully transmit them from generation to generation. For these societies, birth, for example, is a traumatic event, which they try to deal with by the imposition of all kinds of ritual and prohibition (through taboos that are linked to pregnant women, etc.). The child is then given a mark of sexual identity via the act of initiation. Society thus ensures the subject's fertility and its own continuation. Anthropologists stress that initiation is an extremely traumatic event, especially if it happens in adolescence, since before being initiated the subject does not have a clear identity, while after initiation the subject becomes heavily burdened by his or her sexual function and the expectation to perform in accordance with it.[13]

The pre-modern subject has doubts about his or her sexual identity, but the gesture of initiation is supposed to alleviate this doubt and through the cut in the body confirm the subject's sexual identity. This mark on the body is therefore the answer of the big Other, of the symbolic structure, to the subject's dilemma in regard to identity. In the case of the modern subject, we no longer have the inscription of sexual identity on the body, since it is enough that the subject is marked by symbolic castration in his or her inner self. (St. Paul, for example, explains that Christians do not prescribe circumcision, because the subject is already cut in his or her soul.) In modern society, the big Other still has power, since socialization usually proceeds via submission to the symbolic law represented by the paternal authority. By contrast, in contemporary, post-modern society, there has been a radical change in the organization of the family, which also entails a different relation of the subject toward the symbolic order: the return to the ritual of clitoridectomy as well as other forms of inscription on the body (even genital mutilations) in some practices of body art is not the answer of the big Other, but the subject's answer to the non-existence of the big Other.

Before dealing with this return to the cut in the body, let me first try to give a psychoanalytic account of clitoridectomy. The ethnic groups that support this practice usually claim that by cutting the female genitals they protect women's honor and thus show respect for them.[14] The cultures that perform clitoridectomy perceive Western cultures as degenerate, since they do not honor women. Here, we have two totally different points of view about what women's honor is: for Westerners, clitoridectomy is an act that mutilates women and violates human rights, and thus also dishonors women; while for people who embrace clitoridectomy, the absence of this ritual devalues women.

How would psychoanalysis explain this logic of honor and respect for women? Freud dealt with the problem of female shyness, which he linked to the lack, the absence, of a phallus in women. By being shy, the woman tries to cover the lack and to avert the gaze from it. However, this shyness has in itself a phallic character. So it can be said that the very lack of the phallic organ in woman results in the phallicization of her whole body or a special part of the body; and covering up this part of the body has a special, seductive effect.

There is no significant difference between woman's shyness and her honor: "The respect for women means that there is something that should not be seen or touched."[15] Both shyness and respect concern the problem of castration, the lack that marks the subject. The insistence on respect is a demand for distance, which also implies a special relation toward the lack in the other.

Freud thought that woman is the subject who actually lacks something, which means that in her case castration was effective. As a result of this, the woman has *Penisneid* (penis envy). In psychoanalytic practice, women's "deprivation" appears in many forms: as a fantasy of some essential injustice, as inferiority complex, as a feeling of non-legitimacy, as a lack of consistency or a lack of control, or even as a feeling of body fragmentation. The Freudian solution to this "deprivation" was maternity. But for Lacan, women's relation toward the lack is much more complicated: the problem of femininity is not simply linked to having or not having a penis. The lack concerns the subject's very being – both a man and a woman are marked by lack, but they relate differently to this lack. Woman does not cover up the lack by becoming a mother, since, for Lacan, the problem of the lack cannot be solved on the level of having but on the level of being. Motherhood is not a solution to woman's lack, since there is no particular object (not even a child) that can ever fill up this lack.

Respect, therefore, has to do with the subject's relation to the lack in the other, which also means that respect is just another name for the anxiety that the subject feels in regard to this lack. The respect for the father, for example, needs to be understood as a way in which the subject tries to avoid the recognition that the father is actually impotent and powerless – that there is nothing behind his authority. Here, we come again to the problem of castration. Lacan understands castration as something that is linked to the radical emptiness of the subject. The subject is nothing by him or herself; he or she acquires all authority and power only from outside – from symbolic insignias. When we respect the father, we believe that the insignias have real power and thus we cover up the fact that the father is castrated, which means that he is himself an empty and powerless subject.

Respect is therefore an imaginary relationship of the subject toward another subject, or, better, toward the symbolic status that this other subject temporarily assumes. (Of course, respect does not concern only our relationship with another subject, but also with the big Other, the symbolic structure as such. Paying respect to our homeland, the flag, the law, etc., is a subject's imaginary means of taking the big Other as consistent order.)

The modern idea of human rights is based on the Kantian subject. And, especially in the case of human rights, we usually invoke the idea of respect. Human rights concern some part of the subject's inner freedom, which the community or other people have no right to violate. (And here freedom is also meant as protection of the subject's bodily integrity. From this perspective, those who criticize clitoridectomy rightly point out that this practice contradicts the idea of human rights.) If we take into account the aforementioned thesis that respect means the need for a distance toward the lack that marks the subject, the idea of respect that human rights invoke also assumes another meaning. The inner freedom of the subject that human rights protect concerns nothing other than the lack that marks the subject when he or she becomes a speaking being. And when we respect the bodily integrity of the subject, this actually means that we avert our gaze from the fact that the subject actually does not have a naturally given bodily integrity, since this integrity comes into being only when the subject undergoes symbolic castration. Then the subject will be temporarily entrusted with a certain symbolic power, but the lack that pertains to his or her subjectivity will nonetheless remain.

Human rights were invented at the time of the Enlightenment, when European subjects lost their roots in tradition.[16] Subsequent political struggles have conceived human rights in a non-discriminatory way, and today they are based on the principle that the subject should be respected regardless of gender, age, race, etc. Here we have an understanding of respect that greatly differs from that which is embraced by the defenders of clitoridectomy. The latter can respect only a woman who has been initiated and not just any woman. Similarly, some cultures respect women only when they are covered by a veil.

The contemporary understanding of human rights also includes the idea of freedom of choice. A widely held liberal position on clitoridectomy, for example, is that women need to be educated about the torturous nature of the practice: but if an educated woman still insists on being circumcised, then the educators are usually powerless to stop her, concluding: "What can we do? It's her choice." As I demonstrated apropos the Amish case in Chapter 6, education does not simply establish a neutral terrain on which the subject can make a free choice, it also imposes a certain dominant ideology on the subject; just as, on another level, a subject's ethnic community imposes its ideology.

Let us now turn to self-torture in body art. These practices are usually understood as an individual's choice to use his or her body as he or she pleases. However, it is only quite recently that the practices of body mutilation have been perceived as art. How would psychoanalysis explain this change in the perception of what is art? According to the standard criticism of psychoanalysis, psychoanalytic interpretation reduces a work of art or a religious experience to a pathological – perverse, neurotic or even psychotic – formation, to a sublimated expression of some unconscious impetus or conflict, etc. With the help of Lacan's theory, we can answer this criticism by turning around the terms of a "reductionist" interpretive procedure: the problem is not to establish the pathological libidinal roots of a publicly acknowledged symbolic formation (religious vision, work of art, etc.); on the contrary, the question is how the public socio-symbolic space of the "big Other" is structured so that it allows someone who displays the features of psychopathology to acquire the status of a highly esteemed public person? For example, why is it that a woman with features that, in an Oriental culture, result in praise for her as a deep mystic visionary, is in our modern culture dismissed as the hysterical or even psychotic author of hallucinatory ramblings?[17] Why is it that a man who finds intense fulfillment in starving and whipping himself was hailed as an ascetic martyr in early Christianity, while today he appears to us as a masochistic pervert? One can say that the Catholic Church's "wisdom" was to allow a space within its institutionalized ranks for the exercise of the *jouissance féminine* irreducible to the paternal symbolic law (permitting nuns their mystical experiences). And on a different level, the same goes for modern art: for example, why is it that a person piercing his body in public would even a decade ago be dismissed as someone who is exposing an abhorrent private perversion, while today his act is seen as an artistic performance? What a specific culture perceives as art thus always depends on a certain social consensus and not simply on the idea of personal choice.[18] People have always mutilated and tortured themselves, but self-mutilation only came to be understood as an artistic practice and not simply as a masochist's private indulgence when a change occurred in the social symbolic organization.

So what has happened in contemporary society to allow the cut in the body to be perceived as art? A generally accepted thesis is that in today's society the way the subject identifies with the law or, better, with the symbolic order has changed. The dissolution of the traditional family structure changed the subject's relation toward authority, which means that the subject nowadays appears as someone who is in a position to freely choose his or her own identity, including even his or her sexual orientation. In pre-modern society, initiation ritual situates the subject in the social structure and assigns to him or her a special place as well as his or her sexual role. In modern, Enlightenment society, we no longer have initiation rituals, but the authority of the law is still at work. The law is linked to the role of the father; and in taking a position against this law, i.e. by distancing him- or herself from this law, the modern subject acquires "freedom". In contrast, in post-modern society we have a total disbelief in authority and in the power of the symbolic order, the so-called big Other. But this disbelief has not simply resulted in the subject's liberation from the law or other forms of social coercion. The post-modern subject no longer accepts the power of institutions or society's power to fashion his or her identity, and sometimes believes in the possibility of self-creation, maybe in the form of playing with his or her sexual identity or making out of him- or herself a work of art. However, in this process of freeing the subject from the big Other, one can also observe the subject's anger and disappointment in regard to the very authority of the big Other. It thus appears as if it was not the subject who recognized that the big Other does not exist and that the authority is just a fraud, but that the big Other has somehow "betrayed" the subject. The father's authority, for example, revealed itself only as a mask of his impotence, the social rituals in institutions appear more and more as a farce. However, this apparent liberation of the subject from authority can also be understood as a choice "forced" on the subject when he or she acknowledged the impotence of authority.

What does this disbelief in the big Other mean? We always knew that the big Other was just a fiction and that people were somehow pretending when they practiced state, religious or family rituals. Most of the time we believe only that someone else believes in these rituals, which is why we follow them in order to avoid offending others. This belief in the belief of others is well exemplified in parents' pretense that they are playing Santa Claus because children believe in him. But when children find out that Santa Claus is just a fiction, they go on pretending to believe in him, so that they will not offend their parents, who still think that their children believe in Santa Claus. What we have today is precisely the disbelief in the fiction of the big Other. The logic of this disbelief is exemplified in the well-known anecdote from one of the Marx brothers' films. When Graucho Marx was caught in an obvious lie, his response was: "Whom do you believe – my words or your eyes?" The belief in the big Other is the belief in words, even when they contradict one's own eyes. What we have today is therefore precisely a mistrust in mere words (i.e. in the symbolic fiction). People want to see what is behind the fiction.

But the encounter with what is behind the fiction can be most traumatic for the subject. An example of the fictional character of the big Other is the rules of politeness in speech. When we meet someone, we usually say, "How nice to see you", even if we're actually thinking, "Drop dead, I hate you." If we stop using polite words, we do not achieve a simple liberation from the fictional character of politeness, but encounter violence, which radically disrupts social bonds.

Lacan's famous definition of psychosis is that what is excluded from the symbolic returns as the real. Psychotics are the ones who do not identify with the fiction of the symbolic order, since for them the symbolic falls into the real. A psychotic, for example, does not believe in the fictional character of God, but has direct contact with God: he hears the voice of God, God's eyes are constantly pursuing him, etc.

On another level, today's disbelief in the fictional character of the father's authority has caused a return of the father as the real – the father who harasses, abuses children, has insatiable sexual desires, i.e. a father who very much resembles the character of the Freudian father of the primal horde, who was the possessor of all women and denied his sons access to *jouissance*.

Disbelief in the symbolic fiction and the search for the real thing was also obvious at the time of the death of Princess Diana. According to public opinion polls, the majority of British people believe that the monarchy is a relic of the past – an archaic institution that should be either abolished or radically changed. So people no longer believe in the fictional character of the kingdom; however, at the time of Diana's funeral, people were upset that the queen did not show emotion. People wanted her to demonstrate her sorrow, to address the nation and to fly the palace flag at half-mast. On the one hand, therefore, we disbelieve the fiction of monarchy, but, on the other hand, we desperately want the fiction to cease to be a fiction and to see what is behind it – a weeping queen, a change in the centuries-old ritual concerning the flag, etc.

The public identification with Diana also shows the changes that have come about in the way the public identifies with its idols. In the past, idols were supposed to be active for ordinary people who perceived their idols as having abilities they did not have – bravery, intelligence, etc. But Diana was an idol who was passive for the people. Hers greatly resembled the attitude of someone who complains about an institution but is actually part of it, who likes to help others, but does not sacrifice his or her own well-being. If in the past people tended to identify with an idol who was not like them, in the case of Diana they identified with someone who was exactly like them – passive, not too intelligent, etc.

One of the ways in which the subject today deals with the absence of the big Other is by narcissistic self-admiration. The lack of identification with an Ego Ideal (a symbolic role or authority ideal) results in the subject's identification with an imaginary role (i.e. Ideal Ego) in which the subject finds him- or herself likeable. This narcissistic search for the perfect image results in the subject's obsession with changing his or her body with the help of excessive dieting, exercise, plastic surgery, etc. Another aspect of the subject's concern with the non-existence of the big Other is discernible in the contemporary phenomenon of the so-called "culture of complaint". In Western societies nowadays people complain about all kinds of injustices in their private and public lives: they search for culprits, those who have deprived them of their happiness, wealth, respect, etc. Disbelief in the power of the big Other results in the belief that there are various small others (institutions and authorities in the subject's immediate environment) who are guilty of causing trouble in people's lives. And the legal as well as financial compensation that the subject seeks is supposed to reinstall the lost equilibrium, at least for a moment.

Still another reflection of today's disbelief in the big Other is displayed in the aforementioned practices of body art. Isn't this inscription on the body an attempt by the subject to deal with the absence of the big Other? Has the contemporary subject taken initiation into his or her own hands? Before trying to answer these questions, let us first consider the inscription on the body as an attempt to re-establish the father's authority, as exemplified in Peter Greenaway's film, *The Pillow Book*.

The film starts with a little girl, Nagiko, whose face is painted by her father, a calligrapher. The father says that when God created man, he painted his eyes, then his lips, and finally his sex. When God was satisfied with his creation he signed his name on the man's neck, so that he would never forget it. And the father also signs his name on Nagiko when he finishes his painting (Figure 9).

But Nagiko is marked by yet another memory from her childhood. When she was a little girl, she saw how her father humiliated himself in front of the publisher who printed his calligraphy. The publisher was extremely rude and demanded sexual favours from the father; but when the publisher stopped publishing his works, it totally ruined her father.

A grown-up Nagiko finds special enjoyment in lovemaking when her partners write on her body. Men are usually surprised by this demand, and when they comply with it, the written product is not very impressive. When Nagiko meets the young, beautiful Jerome, she decides to reverse the roles and she herself starts writing on Jerome's body. Jerome is also a lover of the now old publisher to whom Nagiko proposes that he publish her book. When the publisher rejects the project, Nagiko starts writing the book on

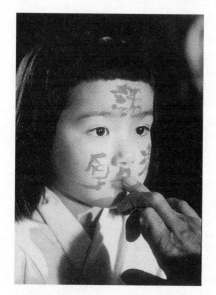

Figures 9, 10, 11 Body paintings from *The Pillow Book*.

Jerome's body. With the text on his body, Jerome goes to see the old publisher and the latter passionately copies the writing (Figure 10).

Nagiko completes thirteen body books on themes from love and desire to suffering and death. One of the books is actually written on Jerome's dead body. When the publisher learns about his lover's death, he excavates Jerome's body and in utter despair copies the book (Figure 11). Outraged by this act, Nagiko writes her last book, "The book of the dead", on the body of a Sumo wrestler, who then kills the publisher. Nagiko has thus finally taken revenge for the humiliation of her father. Since her father was not enough of an authority figure and did not stand up to the publisher, the daughter, using the father's profession of calligraphy, punishes the publisher. This writing on the body needs to be understood as the inscription of the absent law of the father, the mark of the father's symbolic power, an act needed to re-establish his authority.

In the inscription on the body, therefore, we can see a subject's search for the absent law or a re-establishment of the authority of the big Other. Public support for all kinds of religious fundamentalism in contemporary society can also be understood as an attempt to find a coherent big Other. Similarly, the insistence on clitoridectomy by immigrants to Western countries can be taken as a desperate endeavor to identify with some symbolic law that would guarantee the subject's identity. A different kind of search for the law can be found in the masochistic practices of body art.

Some forms of body art can clinically be described as perversions. Of course, the term perversion is not used pejoratively. For psychoanalysis, the pervert is the subject for whom castration has not been fully operative, which is why the subject endlessly searches for the law that might complete castration. Perversion is thus not beyond the law, but an attempt to find the law. And one of the most common forms of perversion is masochism.

A documentary entitled *Sick: The Life and Death of Bob Flanagan, Supermasochist* (Kirby Dick, 1996) deals with the theme of masochism and art. The film depicts the performance artist Bob Flanagan, who enjoys masochistic rituals in which, with the help of his wife/mistress, his skin is cut, his genitals mutilated, etc. It is crucial to the act that the artist suffers an incurable illness, cystic fibrosis, which makes him unable to breathe without an iron lung. The film is a collage of the artist's performances, most of which were presented in art galleries. The film records the artist's death and his corpse being photographed by his devoted wife. The most shocking scene includes the act of genital self-mutilation, in which the artist nails his penis onto a wooden board. When he removes the nails, blood squirts onto the camera. (This scene is hard to watch – many male viewers identify so strongly with the pain of the ritual that they scream in panic, or even leave the room.)[19]

Now, how can one understand artistic enjoyment in masochistic practices? First, it must be pointed out that masochism and sadism never go hand in hand. As Gilles Deleuze pointed out, a masochist and a sadist do not form a couple.[20] A sadist regards himself as the executor of some higher will, an ideal. He sees himself as a mere object through which this ideal finds fulfillment. And a sadist tortures his victims because he is executing the desire of this higher will. The masochist, on the contrary, searches for a torturer whom the masochist himself will instruct (how to beat him, etc.). In the masochistic situation, the victim speaks through the torturer: here, it is therefore not the torturer who invents the forms of punishment; the inventor is the victim himself.

The torturer is usually a woman who takes on the role of the cold, severe mother. The masochist must establish a contract with the torturer that describes in detail the conditions of the torture. The masochist is thus not simply tied by chains but by the power of the contract through which he invests in the torturer the symbolic power of the law. The torturer acts like a cruel mother who humiliates the father figure, who in turn is made incarnate in the victim himself. The masochist therefore invests the law in his mother – in the very object of incestuous enjoyment – and by doing so excludes the father from the symbolic. Paradoxically, the excluded father then returns in the guise of the masochist himself, since the masochist takes on the role of the weak, humiliated father who needs to be punished.

For the masochist, castration has not been completed, which means that the symbolic law did not become fully operative. This is why the masochist, in his ritual torture, caricatures castration and tries to make the law operative through the contract with his mistress. The subject (i.e. the hysteric or the obsessional) for whom the castration was effective is always unsatisfied with the ways in which he or she tries to fill the lack: the subject thus complains about the law that supposedly prevents his or her enjoyment; however, the subject finds a special enjoyment in this very dissatisfaction. But the masochist finds enjoyment in the punishment imposed by the law that he himself establishes. Since he lacks the symbolic prohibition, the masochist becomes his own executioner.

Another example of how contemporary art uses writing on the body is found in Jenny Holzer's work *Lustmord*, which deals with the problem of rape in the Bosnian war.[21] The *Lustmord* project takes pieces of unattributable skin (is this the victim, the perpetrator, the observer or even someone else?) and by writing on them tries to make rape comprehensible (Figures 12, 13, 14). However, although we have three points of view, three accounts of the event, the trauma remains unuttered. Of course, one can easily draw the conclusion here that words cannot recount the traumatic dimensions of such a violent act as rape. But in Holzer's work, the writing on the skin actually exposes the incongruity between the rape as a traumatic act and its symbolic inscription. In Holzer's writings on the skin, it is not that the real of the trauma suddenly came to the surface and thus was inscribed in language. On the contrary, the writings remain somehow detached from the body – they look like painful, incomprehensible messages that can never grasp the trauma of the act of rape. Jenny Holzer's body writings thus show very clearly, on the one hand, that violence is symbolically mediated, but, on the other hand, that it touches the real which cannot be symbolized.

Some might also take Holzer's body writings as a form of violence over the body, as a cut in the body. The question, therefore, is: does Holzer's use of the body differ from that of the artists who masochistically cut their own bodies, tattoo them, or even mutilate their genitals? Writing on the skin, as presented in Jenny Holzer's work, cannot be taken as a perverse search for the law, although the *Lustmord* project does reflect the contemporary disbelief in the big Other. There is no authority here that can help us to understand the logic of rape; there is no point in the symbolic network with which the subject might identify in order to get answers to his or her trauma. We are left with an utterly fragmented corpus of texts written on the skin, and neither the text nor the reality of the skin give ground to the subject. With the non-existence of the big Other who would dress the subject with an identity, we come to the point where the subject necessarily becomes the designer of his or her own story, and the only material available to the subject is his or her own skin.

The *Lustmord* project and some masochist forms of body art resemble each other in their reflection of contemporary disbelief in the big Other. However, the crucial difference between the two projects is that the masochists constantly try to re-establish the big Other through laws that they themselves invent, while Holzer recognizes the fact that the big Other does not exist, but does not try to cover up the fact. This insistence on the

Figures 12, 13, 14 Jenny Holzer, *Lustmord.* (© 1994 Jenny Holzer. Courtesy of Jenny Holzer Studio, New York.)

emptiness of the symbolic order makes Holzer's art much more heroic than the masochists' cuts in the body.

How, therefore, can one understand the turn to perversion in contemporary art? My point is not that the use of the body in art signals some kind of generalized perversion of our society. If a masochist castrating himself on the stage is clinically a pervert, this is not the case for the majority of artists who use their bodies in art work. Similarly, one cannot universally take body piercing and tattooing as clinical forms of perversion. Most of those who in one way or another mark their bodies would fall more into the clinical category of neurosis than perversion; their acts are an imitation of perversion and not an actual perversion. But, what is the difference between perverts and neurotics who just imitate perversion? Both of them stage some kind of drama when they paint or mutilate their bodies. The perverts stage this drama in order to deny castration: via their masochistic ritual, they mock castration, while at the same time this very staging is also an attempt to find a law which would complete castration. In the case of perverts, castration is thus first denied, and then mockingly staged as an outside event, which does not touch the subject in his or her inner being, but behind this is a failed attempt to make castration operative again. Neurotics, on the contrary, stage perverse rituals in order to come to terms with the lack that has been introduced by castration. Since for neurotics castration was effective, they create a fantasy scenario to cover up the lack, which is the result of castration; i.e. they try to show how they are not essentially marked by the law, since they can openly play with castration rituals on the stage.

WHAT LIES BEHIND IMAGINARY SIMULACRA?

The fact that subjects face a radical rejection of belief in the big Other, or that they know that the big Other actually does not exist, does not mean that the symbolic structure is not operative. Subjects are still strongly marked by the symbolic prohibition although they might no longer identify with the authorities who are supposed to be bearers of this prohibition.

The symbolic structure today seems more and more often to have been replaced by imaginary simulacra with which a subject identifies. Life is like a computer game in which the subject can play with his or her identity, can randomly follow fashion rituals, has no strong national or religious beliefs, etc. But the fact that life appears as a screen on which everything is changeable has resulted in a desperate search for the real behind the fiction. The cut in the body thus appears as an escape from the imaginary simulacra that dominate our society.

Young people usually explain their obsession with tattooing and body piercing as ways to escape the pressures of the dominant fashion industry. The media constantly bombard them with images of beauty, and one of the ways to oppose this enforced identification is to perform a real action – to mark the body in a way that cannot be changed.

In recent years, social theory has widely discussed the issue of identity, which appears not only as something socially constructed, but also as something multiform and changeable. Discussions on performativity and sexual difference have also created the impression that the subject can play with his or her sexual identity. The paradox of contemporary cuts in the body is that they seem, at the same time, to be a realization of these theoretical beliefs and a reaction against them. Making a cut in the body does not mean that the subject is merely playing with his or her identity; by irreversibly marking the body, the subject also protests against the ideology that makes everything changeable. The body thus appears as the ultimate point of the subject's identity. Since the subject does not want to simply play with the imaginary simulacra presented by the dominant fashion ideologies, he or she tries to find in the body the site of the real.

For the artists on the group Body Radicals,[22] the body is today the only remaining realm over which an individual has retained power. "Unmediated, direct access to the inner being through the artist's own blood or the feeling of pain opens up almost Artaud-like perspectives. What is happening is literal. There is no simulation. The symbolic field of the art is collapsing, bodies become black holes into which symbolic significance implodes."[23] The latter thesis is a very pretentious one, since the Body Radicals call themselves artists and their work is usually presented in art galleries: they may not be accepted by the mainstream art community, but they nonetheless want to be recognized in the alternative spaces of the "symbolic field of art". This demand for social recognition in itself proves that, in the new forms of body art, we are not dealing with some kind of generalized psychosis or with the total collapse of the symbolic order. However, the use of the body in contemporary art does address the subject's problem in searching for something real in the form of his or her body.

Although the artists in the group Body Radicals use their bodies in very different ways in their work, one can find some similarities between them. For the purpose of my analysis here, I will focus only on the work of Orlan[24] and Stelarc.

Orlan's art consists primarily of multiple plastic-surgery operations on her face, which are recorded and, with a commentary in her own voice, presented in art galleries. When Orlan provides theory about her art, her primary point is that she uses her body as a site of public debate. Her art challenges current standards of beauty, it explores the variety of body images that are outside the norms and dictates of the dominant ideology. When she plays with images of femininity, her intention is to practice a transsexuality of woman to woman, which, however, does not follow the usual transsexual desire to have a defined identity. Orlan also claims that, with the help of surgery, one can bring the internal image closer to the external one; she therefore does not need to identify with the image that nature has given her. With the help of surgery, her body is transformed into language ("flesh becomes word"). Orlan plans to be mummified after her death and placed in an art gallery.

Orlan therefore plays with multiple identities; she makes her body a changeable work of art, and by doing so hopes to achieve some kind of immortality. She regards her work as a self-portrait, which is presented as an inscription in the flesh made with the help of the new technologies. Her intention is to impose control not only over her naturally given body image, but also to manipulate the new technologies (like plastic surgery) and use them against the ideals of the dominant ideology.

When Orlan objects to the suggestion that she is performing some kind of self-mutilation, she comes very close to the defenders of clitoridectomy. She claims that her body transformation augments her power and does not diminish it. Similarly, the defenders of clitoridectomy say that the ritual of circumcision actually gives women power they did not have before initiation. And when Orlan says that she transforms her body into language, she caricatures initiation rituals, which in their own ways also mark the body with language.[25]

If, in a pre-modern society, initiation has a very specific role in assigning the subject his or her sexual identity and in imposing a mark of social prohibition on to the body, one cannot say that, in post-modern society, initiation rituals still play the same role. The insistence on clitoridectomy in the case of African immigrants in the West or among very developed

African countries, for example, can be understood as a specific answer to the deadlocks of contemporary society. The class antagonisms in post-industrial society, the globalization of capital, the erosion of tradition, all brought subjects to search for some stable forms of identity. African immigrants may still respect their grandmothers enough to allow them to perform the act of initiation, while they have an utter mistrust of other authorities in the society they live in. Here, we also have a case of disbelief in the fiction of the big Other in contemporary society; thus the insistence on old rituals of initiation must be understood as an answer to this disbelief, i.e. as an attempt to find in the body a place for a stable identity.

When body artists caricature initiation rituals or play with the same new forms of tribalism, they are trying to challenge precisely the idea of a stable identity, while nonetheless trying to find in the body some piece of the real. In their own way, the body artists are also dealing with the deadlocks in contemporary society: with cuts in the body, they challenge the idea that it can give the subject the basis for an identity. So they are actually searching for what is supposed to be behind the body. If it is just a playground for various identities, what is real here?

For Orlan, what is finally unchangeable is the voice. With the help of her voice, she tries to provide explanations for her art: she thus reads from theoretical texts as her face is cut and comments on the surgical procedure. But behind this search for meaning for her changeable face, her voice remains a constant. Orlan's voice is the drive, i.e. the real, that stays the same throughout her performances. Plastic surgery on her face is painful to watch; for viewers it is not only shocking to see her skin being detached from her face, but also to hear her monotonous voice reciting texts at the same time. If Orlan were to be silent, observers might be able to pretend they were seeing a deeply anestheticized, as if dead, person being cut on a stage. In this case, the shock for viewers would not be so very different from the effects of watching horror movies: when one does not want to see a scary scene in a film, one simply closes one's eyes. Of course, in horror movies one still hears the music and the screams, but the voice without the picture is less frightening, since the voice loses its power when it is not accompanied by a picture. But with Orlan, it is the voice that is the real site of horror. If one listens to her voice and keeps one's eyes shut, one does not find relief, since Orlan's voice is a sign of deadliness and of life at the same time. As such, as discussed in Chapter 3, the voice is a death drive that always undermines the subject's identity. Orlan tries to show with her art how she can play with her identity, but her voice nonetheless remains the real, what is in her more than herself (her plastic Self).

Some other artists are trying to find a piece of the real beyond the skin with the help of computer technology and in this endeavor they also try to give up on the human voice and replace it with computerized sound. The Australian artist Stelarc, for example, questions the role of the body in the post-industrial age. His thesis is that, with new developments in technology, the body has become obsolete, since it is biologically ill-equipped to match the technological level of contemporary society. Stelarc wants to create some kind of new meta-body, which first needs to pacify and anesthetize the existing body; i.e. with the help of genetic technology, the organs become replaceable, the skin more durable, the body starts acting without expectation, it produces movements without memory, has no desires, etc. In this way, the self can be placed beyond the skin and connects itself with the virtual world. The body becomes a phantom, which plays with its images and connects itself with the immortal machinery. Reproduction is redesigned, and sexual intercourse is replaced with the interface between the subject and the machine. We no longer have to deal with birth or death. Stelarc thus wants to make life eternal. Although in the end, this life would be nothing but a symbolic fiction, the fiction would nonetheless eliminate the trauma of the unsymbolizable real. As such, life would cease to be life, too.

Both interventions in the body – clitoridectomy and some practices of body art – pose numerous questions about the subject in the post-modern world. Some see the main problem of contemporary society in the total erosion of the symbolic network, which results in some kind of a generalized perversion or even psychosis. Others take the dissolution of the patriarchal system of social authorities as a possibility for subjects to form their own identities without submitting themselves to the imposed normative ideals. But the changed relation of the subject to the symbolic order in contemporary society should be taken neither as a total catastrophe nor as an opening up of unlimited possibilities of freedom. The disbelief in the big Other has, on the one hand, incited people's return to such cruel initiation rituals as clitoridectomy, and, on the other hand, instigated a body art of self-imposed cuts. But is this the only way to respond to the fact that the big Other does not exist? Aren't there other ways of dealing with the inconsistency of the symbolic order?

NOTES

1. For a detailed account of post-modernity, see Fredric Jameson, *Postmodernism, or the Cultural Logic of Late Capitalism,* London: Verso 1993.
2. United Nations data show that there are 130 million women in the world today whose genitals have been mutilated. This practice is widespread in Africa, in some Asian countries and among some immigrants from these places in the West.
3. Although clitoridectomy is prevalent in communities that practice Islam, this ritual is not particular to Islam, much less prescribed by the Koran. In the past, clitoridectomy was sometimes also performed by Catholics, Protestants and Copts, among other religions. The Catholic Church never officially distanced itself from clitoridectomy: missionaries in Africa, for example, did not condemn it. Only the Anglican Church, in the 1920s, denounced the ritual and advised its missionaries to prevent it. See Efua Dorkenoo, *Cutting the Rose: Female Genital Mutilation – The Practice and its Prevention,* London: Minority Rights Publication 1994. See also, Martine Lefeuvre-Deotte, *L'Excision en procès: un différend culturel?,* Paris: L'Harmattan 1997, and Jean-Thierry Maertens, *Le Corps sexionné,* Paris: Aubier 1978.

   Clitoridectomy was also practiced in Europe in the nineteenth century to treat female hysteria. See Jane Ussher, *Women's Madness: Misogyny as Mental Illness,* Hemel Hempstead: Harvester/Wheatsheaf 1991.
4. A court in Cairo recently abolished the prohibition of clitoridectomy in public and private hospitals. Some Egyptian officials also want to erase from school books passages describing the negative effects of clitoridectomy. The Egyptian government had banned clitoridectomy after the death of several girls, but the ban was criticized as being contrary to Islam. See *Marie Claire,* May 1997.
5. Westerners have been powerless in the past to educate people who perform clitoridectomies about the danger of the practice, so now some Westerners, to make clitoridectomy more hygienic, insist that it should be performed in hospitals.

   Some commentators, who do not want to totally condemn clitoridectomy and who see it as part of African culture, are advocating ways to legally regulate it. Morayo Atoki makes such an attempt in her article "Should Female Circumcision Continue to Be Banned?" (*Feminist Legal Studies* 3:2 (August 1995), pp. 223–35). Her point is that clitoridectomy already has its foundations in African jurisprudence, "where the female genitalia is perceived as a symbolic organ that connotes purity and fecundity. Indeed, it is on the female genitalia that two important concepts of

African jurisprudence, 'virginity' and 'fertility', are based. Contracts of marriage and family patterns in many African societies are structured entirely on these two concepts" (ibid., p. 225). The female genitals need to be re-created in a form that indicates their purity. Women's purity has economic value, since it determines the dowry. Atoki also points out that Africans have a different perception of sexuality than Westerners. In Africa, the circumcision of men and women is done to prepare them for, not to deter them from, sexual activity. Circumcision is thus supposed to enhance sexual pleasure by removing the prepuce, while excision is supposed to enhance femininity, and infibulation is carried out to delay sexual intercourse until marriage. The problem with this argument, which tries to find a basis for clitoridectomy in the cultural difference of Africa, is that it nonetheless relies on Western perceptions. Thus, on the one hand, Atoki claims that sexuality in Africa is linked to fertility and not orgasm ("It is the fecundity of a woman which gives her sexuality": p. 231), but, on the other hand, she states that orgasm is not simply a biological experience and that there are other erogenous zones besides the clitoris, like the mouth, the neck, the breast, the ears. So, Africans do not care about orgasm, but even if they do, they already know (what Western feminism has taught us) that orgasm is not a biological fact. Atoki's argument becomes even more confusing when she speaks about the need to preserve the freedom of choice of African women to perform clitoridectomy and to make the procedure legally regulated. Her conclusion is thus that clitoridectomy should be carried out in accordance with law. Atoki's first thesis was that, as a ritual that preserves fertility, clitoridectomy is already part of African jurisprudence. It is thus some kind of cornerstone on which marriage contracts and family patterns are based, i.e. it can also be understood as something that secures the basis of the law itself. As a ritual that provides a foundation for the very existence of community (its fertility), clitoridectomy is regarded as a secret act. Now, how does one apply Western standards of choice and legal regulation to this secret ritual? And if clitoridectomy is already part of African jurisprudence (even its cornerstone), on what basis could Western legal standards collide with African law?

6. Significant is the case of Sierra Leone, one of the poorest countries in Africa, where 90 per cent of women have their genitals mutilated. This ritual is usually conducted in a ceremony in which women secretly go into the bush, where they drink and dance and initiate young girls through the ritual of clitoridectomy. Women take this ritual as something that helps their tradition to survive. And at the same time it is supposed to be the last moment of freedom for women, since after they get married, they live in extremely oppressive conditions. The few women in Sierra Leone who oppose clitoridectomy try to find ways to keep the ritual of women

gathering together once a year to dance and drink, without performing initiation. This suggestion is much criticized in Sierra Leone, since people perceive clitoridectomy as a way of rejecting the strong influence of Western cultures on Sierra Leone society. (See *New York Times*, 31 January 1997.)

7. Note that so-called female circumcision is the mildest of the deformations of female genitals, since circumcision removes only the prepuce that covers the clitoris. Much more severe and also much more widespread is so-called excision, which removes the whole of the clitoris. Even more common and painful is the ritual of infibulation, which means the removal of the clitoris and the labia. After this procedure, the woman's genitals are sewn together and only a small opening is left for the discharge of urine and menstrual blood. This practice causes the death of many women: some women die because they become infected during the procedure (many are also infected by HIV); others develop serious illnesses because their menstrual blood cannot be properly discharged. During her first sexual encounter, a man opens up the woman by cutting the scar, and when the woman is inseminated, she is sewn back. Childbirth is extremely painful for such a woman, since her genitals must be cut once again, which causes numerous infections and sometimes even death.

8. The Mossi of Burkina Faso, as well as the Bambara and Dogon of Mali, believe that the clitoris is dangerous to the child and that if the clitoris touches the child's head during birth it can cause its death.

9. See Dorkenoo, *Cutting the Rose*, p. 25.

10. The defenders of clitoridectomy who invoke its esthetic dimension usually say that it should be compared with the Western obsession with beauty, which leads women to undergo painful plastic surgery, tattooing, etc.

11. On the paradoxical role of men in some pre-modern societies, see Suzette Heald, "Every Man a Hero: Oedipal Themes in Gisu Circumcision", in *Anthropology and Psychoanalysis: An Encounter Through Culture*, ed. Suzette Heald and Ariane Deluz, London: Routledge 1994, and Maurice Bloch, *From Blessing to Violence: History and Ideology in the Circumcision Ritual of the Merina of Madagascar*, Cambridge: Cambridge University Press 1986.

12. See Max Horkheimer, "Authority and the Family", in *Critical Theory: Selected Essays*, New York: Continuum 1972.

13. On the trauma of male circumcision, see Henrietta Moore, "Anthropology and Initiation", *New Formations* 35 (1998).

14. Efua Dorkenoo points out that many African ethnic groups take honor as a collective property of the family: if one member of the family loses his or her pride, the whole family is dishonored. In some communities, the sexual promiscuity of a woman is perceived as something that degrades her husband and justifies his severely punishing his wife when she is unfaithful.

The claim is also made that, once women's honor has been lost, nothing can restore it. (See Dorkenoo, *Cutting the Rose*.)

15. Jacques-Alain Miller, "Des semblants dans la relation entre les sexes", in *La Cause Freudienne* 36 (1997), p. 8.

16. More on human rights is to be found in Chapter 8 of my *The Spoils of Freedom: Psychoanalysis and Feminism after the Fall of Socialism*, London: Routledge 1994.

17. Catherine Clément and Sudhur Kakar published a provocative study of such a case, *La Folie et le saint*, Paris: Editions du Seuil 1993.

18. See Jacques Lacan, *Ethics of Psychoanalysis*, London: Routledge 1993.

19. One feels a similar horror when observing in the media the pictures of mutilated women's genitals. But I do not claim that both practices, clitoridectomy and genital self-mutilation in body art, are similar. It is obvious that in the two cases we have a different logic of choice involved— if one can at all speak about choice in the case of circumcised women. Some might claim that both forms of genital mutilation have in common an esthetic dimension: Flanagan makes a work of art out of his body; and some interpreters regard clitoridectomy as an esthetic practice intended to beautify a woman's body.

20. See Gilles Deleuze, *Masochism: Coldness and Cruelty*, New York: Zone Books 1991.

21. Many contemporary women artists are dealing with the dilemma of the relationship between language and violence. Sue Williams, for example, in her project *Irresistible* (1992) exhibits a mannequin doll that looks like a woman being beaten and on whose body we read the violent sentences uttered by her perpetrator, e.g.: "Look what you made me do", "I think you like it", etc. Shirin Neshat photographs Iranian women covered by headscarves, who hold in their arms a pistol or a gun and whose faces, palms or feet are covered with inscriptions from women's literature. (See her projects: *Unveiling Series [1993], Women of Allah [1994], Under Duty [1994].*) (For an account of the contemporary art that uses writing on the body, see the catalogue *Auf den Leib geschrieben*, Vienna: Kunsthalle Wien im Museumquartier 1995.)

Sue Williams and Shirin Neshat present, on the one hand, a woman who is a passive object of male violence and whose body is marked by male words, and, on the other hand, women who are also oppressed by patriarchal culture, but who resist this structure with a gun and with their own literature. When Jenny Holzer takes the issue of violence and writing, however, she further complicates matters. In Holzer's art we do not have women who are simply objects of male violence or women who try to act against this violence. What Holzer presents are three completely different points of view in regard to rape: that of the perpetrator, the victim and the observer. It is crucial here that one cannot discern the position from which the artist herself speaks. One can guess that, at one and the same time, she speaks from all three positions and from none of them.

By presenting three accounts of rape, Holzer does not fall into the trap of showing the different perspectives as simply incomprehensible to one another, since each of the texts tells the story from a different point of view. Holzer's writing shows that the other is not incomprehensible because of one's ignorance, but because of the radical impossibility of comprehending the perspective of the other, as well as of "feeling" his or her pain. What accounts for this impossibility? The most horrible violence that happens to a subject is usually not physical pain, but violence that destroys the subject's identity, i.e. his or her self-perception. Psychoanalysis teaches us that this self-perception is structured like a fantasy. Fantasy here is not synonymous with illusion, but means a scenario that helps the subject to mask the lack, the so-called Lacanian real (which can also be understood as a trauma), which shatters the subject's very being. The most horrible violence happens when the subject is touched in his or her inner being in such a way that the story that he or she tells him or herself no longer makes sense. When the subject's fantasy has been ruined, he or she might consider him or herself as being just a pile of bones covered by flesh and skin. This subject has no identity anymore and is desperately trying to fashion a new story about him or herself that would also give meaning to the traumatic event. (On violence and fantasy, see Chapter 1 in my *The Spoils of Freedom*.) For an extended analysis of Jenny Holzer's art, see my commentary in *Jenny Holzer*, London: Phaidon 1998.

22. The group Body Radicals includes artists like Orlan, Ron Athey, Stelarc, Franko B and Annie Sprinkle. While they all use their own bodies as their means of expression, their art and the explanations they give for it differ significantly.

23. See Body Radicals' home page on the Internet.

24. For an analysis of Orlan's art, see also Parveen Adams, *The Emptiness of the Image*, London: Routledge 1995.

25. Ron Athey and Franko B also caricature various forms of initiation rituals in their performances, in which they primarily play with blood, shit and other bodily discharges.

    Some forms of body art, as well as the use of blood and excreta, were widespread already in the sixties and seventies; however, the "actionist" strategy of the artists like Valie Export and Peter Weibel is incompatible with today's body-art performances. For an overview of various practices of body art, see Amelia Jones, *Body Art/Performing the Subject*, Minneapolis: Minnesota University Press 1998.

CONCLUSION:
"THIS SAYS NOTHING"

People resort to all kinds of self-help manuals to put their love lives in order. *The Rules*, a recent bestseller, gives women guidelines for seducing men: a woman must make herself elusive and unavailable to incite a man's desire. A man must be allowed to be a chaser and a woman must restrain herself and make herself hard to get. *The Rules* strongly advises a woman not to call a man she is interested in, not to accept his last-minute invitation for a date, not to show him too much attention and, especially, not to sexually consummate the relationship before it is clear that the man is fully committed to her. These instructions sound like the old-fashioned patriarchal moral codes that mothers have long preached to their daughters, but they are not a simple return to an old tradition. *The Rules* acknowledges the fact that today we no longer have paternal authorities who encourage women to be mysterious and restrain themselves when they meet a man for the first time. In contrast to past generations, most women today are willing to pursue men and are also not shy about having sex with them early in a relationship. Feminism brought significant changes to women's lives, which they are not willing to give up in order to find "true" love. But the extinction of old sexual prohibitions has not make people's love lives any easier. Love today remains a matter of seduction. What is in the subject more than him or herself is still the object that incites passionate attachments. And as Chapter 1 showed, barriers and symbolic prohibitions greatly contribute to the attractiveness of the love-object. Since today most people reject patriarchal ideas of courtship and are not willing to return to past rituals of seduction, the authors of *The Rules* decided to offer a feminist version of the old prohibitions.

The book was such a success that the authors went on to establish a whole movement for "Rules girls": advice on the Internet, women's support groups, etc. For example, a woman who is tempted to contact a man she likes can get in touch with a Rules support group, where other women will help her to restrain herself and not call the man. But what does a woman do when she finally succeeds in her seduction? For the authors of *The Rules*, marriage is still the most desirable goal a woman can pursue. But even when married, the woman needs to keep herself elusive and not too available. To this end, women can now turn to new guidelines in the form of *The Rules 2*, a book that aims to be politically correct, offering rules for homosexual couples too.

How can we understand this search for rules? Although the new guidelines for seduction are similar in content to the old ones, there is nonetheless a significant difference between them. In the past, the codes of seduction were deeply embedded in traditional mores, while today they appear as something one invents: rules are thus understood as mere technical devices that may help women to achieve a desired goal – to find a partner. This change from the old courtship rituals to new rules must be understood in the context of the changed relationship of the subject toward authorities and the symbolic order in general, which the last chapter analyzed.

Subjects today play with their identities and do not allow any authority to fashion their lives; but at the same time, they desperately search for new guidelines to bring some "order" into this free play with identities. One finds examples of this search for new rules not only in seduction, but also in the public debates about cyberspace and genetic science.

Cyberspace initially seemed to open up unlimited possibilities of new forms of communication, but then questions arose about moral rules and the function of law. How can law decide what is allowed and what is prohibited in cyberspace? Can a written attack sent on the Internet be understood as rape? How does computer-fashioned child pornography differ from pornography that uses live children? Another complicated legal case is posed when a person enters someone else's computer system, steals his or her fictional name and then uses a written message to sexually attack a third party. What is rape here: the first attack, which concerns the takeover of another's identity, the written sexual attack, or both?

One finds a similar search for rules in the debates about genetic engineering. With the new developments in genetic cloning it may be possible in the future to create a new human being out of the genetic material of a dead one. If until now subjects utterly feared death, in the future, eternal life will become something to be frightened of. Eternal life will resemble the Lacanian death drive – the force that is the remainder of symbolization but which also constantly undermines the symbolic order that tries to keep it at bay. Since we fear that such indestructible life might be the future product of developments in science, we desperately seek some control over research with the help of new guidelines devised by various ethical committees.

How can we understand this search for new rules? Theorists who analyze the new risks that accompany scientific development point out that society today "becomes a laboratory, but there is no one responsible for its outcomes".[1] Scientific research in bioengineering and the nuclear industry, for example, can bring radical changes in the organization of society and in people's lives; but there is no authority to control the risks created in the interplay of science, social institutions and politics.

The traditional patriarchal type of family with a strong father figure is in decline in today's developed countries. Although many conservatives want to return to this form of family organization, there is no way back.[2] But, paradoxically, the new types of corporation are trying to replace the old family structures. Of course, we cannot simply say that managers have become the new patriarchal father figures.[3] On the contrary, corporations present themselves as institutions with no one in charge: they are usually led by benevolent, permissive-seeming authorities who hold all the strings in their hands but do not externally appear to be authority figures.

Douglas Coupland's *Microserfs* depicts how such benevolent authorities function in a corporation like Microsoft.[4] Paradoxically, Microsoft named its business complex a "campus", thus pretending to be just another type of educational institution concerned about the public good and not primarily interested in profit. The ideology of this corporation relies on the myth of youth: a good hacker has to be young, and hackers over the age of thirty-five are perceived as being far too old to compete with younger ones. For employees, there is no life outside the corporation: they also work at weekends, live mostly in communal houses near the campus, socialize among themselves, and compete primarily about who will be more productive, richer and, of course, get close to Bill Gates.[5] He is referred to by his first name, Bill, since he presents himself as a brother[6] – a young, enthusiastic hacker. But behind this benevolent image is a cruel figure who randomly punishes or rewards his subordinates. Bill thus initially looks like an Ideal with whom young hackers easily identify, while at the same time functioning as a superego, i.e. as a master who invisibly controls his employees and constantly makes them feel guilty for not being productive enough. It is always a mystery to the employees why Bill promotes some and fires others. And the employees' greatest fear is to receive an e-mail from Bill, since it can contain the most punitive as well as the most rewarding message.

This new type of corporation greatly relies on the fact that the subject's relation to authority has changed in contemporary society. The corporation's executives know that young people are not willing to simply submit themselves to the will of the authorities at their workplace, but primarily want to do creative work, i.e. they want to express themselves in their work. A corporation like Microsoft plays on precisely this desire to be creative. When Microsoft searches for new cadres among college students, it is not primarily interested in hiring the students with the best marks, but those who have the desire to invent and are willing to explore something new in life. The best recruits are those with slightly eccentric intellectual or artistic interests, and who also reject traditional authorities.

The corporation relies on the fact that most youngsters today live in very permissive environments: even college functions as an extended form of the permissive family, where the teachers are benevolent surrogate parents. The corporation presents itself as just another type of permissive institution, where employees will go on living a kind of student life while being paid for playing with computers. But when new employees become part of the corporate machinery, they quickly realize the cruelty of the logic of capital that governs the corporation. It presents itself as a new type of cosy family – but only to increase its profits. Young employees look forward to the prospect of not being forced to "grow up", of continuing to enjoy the security of the family-like institutions that have pampered them throughout their lives, but when they lose their initial creativity, problems arise: they feel guilty for not being productive enough and fear losing their jobs. Young hackers are thus hired to be themselves – unruly youngsters with lots of creative ideas. They are then placed in a non-traditional work environment that looks like a relaxed computer playground. But, once integrated into the corporation, they often lose the eccentric qualities that made them desirable employees in the first place. The fact that a subject has lost his or her creative edge and thus cannot fulfill the "desire" of the institution can easily cause a psychological breakdown and bring the hacker's computer career to an early end.

The new authorities thus function as superego figures who disguise themselves as benevolent doubles of their subordinates. The new authorities are hard to recognize as such; and for subordinates it is also hard to guess what the authorities actually require of them. This uncertainty about who the authority is and what it wants contributes to the subjects' feeling of being at a loss in today's society. And one of the ways to deal with this non-transparency of authorities is to establish some kind of ersatz authority structures like support groups or ethical committees, which help to create the illusion that the subjects themselves can "take charge". Isn't the search for new rules and the establishment of multiform ethical committees linked to the fact that, globally, not much can be changed in society, since big capital is increasingly independent of politics? Here, the point is not to oppose the establishment of ethical committees that discuss the impact of science; rather, it is to remember that only control over big capital can limit the risks science generates. The crucial political problem is thus how to control capital and not simply how to limit the risks of scientific development.

There is a certain similarity between a capitalist superpower like the United States and the ancient Roman Empire. In the last crisis years of the Empire, people turned inward and engaged in "care of the self". Similarly today, when power relations are opaque and authorities disguised, people are absorbed in changing their self-images, playing with their identities, etc. The subject's incentive to change his or her body is thus a way of dealing with an increasing powerlessness in the face of changes that affect society at large.

If, as the introduction to this book showed, the ideology of high fashion insists on the uniqueness of the subject, who has no need to dress up like someone else but must only enhance his or her individuality (with the help of minimalist, but expensive clothes), i.e. be him- or herself, the ideology of the new technologies like cybertechnology or genetic engineering presents the subject with the possibility of being another person. The subject is thus encouraged simultaneously to take his or her individuality as a treasure to be brought to the surface (with the right clothes, of course), and to explore a change in his or her individuality by adopting a new identity in cyberspace, by changing his or her face with the help of plastic surgery and by genetically altering his or her body. What does it mean for the subject to simply be him- or herself, or to try to be someone else?

The problems inherent in such possible changes of identity are vividly presented in the film *Face/Off* (John Woo, 1997), which deals with the relationship between the detective Archer (John Travolta) and the criminal Castor (Nicholas Cage), who has killed Archer's son. To get even for this crime and to prevent another of Castor's criminal plans, Archer decides to use a new technology that allows the individual to take on the face of someone else. Castor is thus secretly captured and his face is transferred to Archer's skull, but then Castor also succeeds in persuading the doctors to put Archer's face on him. Both men are thus caught in the image of each other, and for each the worst horror is to see himself in the mirror. At the end of the film, each tries to kill the other to get back his own face. In the last duel, when it becomes clear that Archer will win the battle, the main question is whether he will also be able to reappropriate his face in undamaged form. In the midst of his death throes, Castor still desperately tries to damage his face, so that Archer will remain stuck with Castor's face.

Archer's horror at having the enemy's face must be read in the context of his relationship with his daughter. At the beginning of the film, he constantly wonders why his teenage daughter cannot simply be herself but always uses excessive make-up, colors her hair, dresses like a punk, etc. When Archer and Castor fight in front of the daughter, however, she cannot decide who is really her father. Archer, who now has Castor's face, says that his voice should assure her that he is her father, while Castor, who has Archer's face, persuades her that she should simply believe her eyes. The daughter follows Castor's suggestion and fires the gun at her real father.

This dilemma of choice between voice and appearance shows how the voice designates the subject much more than his or her appearance does. Here again we have confirmation that the voice is what in the subject is more than him or herself. The voice is also the site of authority; thus, when the daughter does not listen to her father's voice, she is actually rebelling against his authority. In the past, the father had demanded that she stop disguising her face; but later the daughter believes the father's mask more than his voice, thus in some way mocking his belief that one should present a natural image. This distinction between the face and the voice is similar to that in Orlan's art. As pointed out in the last chapter, Orlan might radically change her face, but what makes her unique and in some way always the same is her unchanged voice. But this voice also tells us what to make of her art. Thus, when Orlan speaks during her operations and tries to create meaning for her art, her voice also becomes a voice of authority.

At the end of *Face/Off*, Archer kills Castor and thus gets his face back. Afterwards, Archer's family is reunited and for the first time we see the daughter without make-up, as if finally she too has stopped pretending to be someone else. But the family finds itself with another member: they are joined by Castor's orphaned son. Paradoxically, the murderer's son replaces Archer's dead son and the two boys even look similar. If, finally, Archer and his daughter became who they are, Castor's son pays for his father's crime by becoming someone else, since it is only when Castor's son replaces the dead boy that the family's trauma is finally forgotten.[7]

The film deals with the idea of a future technology that will allow the subject to radically alter his or her body; but the conclusion is that it is better to remain who one is. Although Archer needs to masquerade with the enemy's face in order to punish the original possessor of this face, his actual power comes from what he is beyond the face – a righteous man who loves his family. This film thus tries to convince us that regardless of the developments of medical technology, what still matters most for humans is the difference between good and evil – and this concerns what the subject is beyond his or her face.

If *Face/Off* envisions a society in which one is able to transplant faces, the science-fiction thriller *Gattaca* (Andrew Niccol, 1997) goes a step further and asks what happens to the subject's identity in a genetically controlled society. Here, parents can decide whether their child will be tall or short, have a high IQ or other desirable traits. As a geneticist tells some expectant parents: "The child is still yours, but simply the best of you." Such a genetically perfected person becomes a member of the privileged class of Valids, while those who are born in a natural way, without genetic interventions, are the underclass In-Valids. Vincent (Ethan Hawke), an In-Valid with poor vision and a congenital heart disease, wants to become an astronaut, although his genetic code does not allow him to do so. Using an illegal DNA broker, he makes a deal with Jerome (Jude Law), who has the right genes but has been paralyzed in an accident. Jerome provides Vincent with blood, urine samples and an identity, while Vincent has Jerome's dreams and desires. After he overcomes numerous obstacles, even an accusation of murder, Vincent finally succeeds in his aim and, under Jerome's name, is accepted for the space mission, while the real Jerome commits suicide.

Gattaca thus addresses important questions like: What is it about us that makes us who we are? Can each person's potential be determined from a drop of blood? Are we the sum of our genes, i.e. are our traits coded into our cells, or is there something deeper and more mysterious that allows us to overcome our genetic constraints? Jerome provides the answer to these questions when he says: "I got a better end of the deal. I only lent you my body, but you lent me your dreams." What makes genes operative is thus the subject's desire. This is also alluded to in the film's epigraph: "There is no gene for the human spirit"; which is supposed to give us hope that the future will be less grim than expected.

Both *Gattaca* and *Face/Off* deal with the influence of science on human life in the near future. The films similarly depict how a subject always needs his double to bring out what is in him more than himself. *Face/Off* plays with the distinction between the good and the bad man, only to show that the good man needs to internalize some character traits of the bad one in order to become more "human". Before Archer takes on his enemy's face, he was distant toward his family and his colleagues, had no passions, etc., while Castor was excessive in his enjoyment of sex, money and crime. When their change of identity is finally resolved and Archer gets back his face, he nonetheless keeps some of Castor's spirit: he becomes cheerful and passionate, more loving toward his family and friends. As in *Gattaca*, where Jerome's genetic material becomes "alive" because of Vincent's enthusiasm, in *Face/Off*, the reserved Archer becomes a better man after the interaction with Castor.

In both films, however, we have a crucial surplus factor at work in the play of doubles. In *Face/Off*, Travolta plays a timid righteous man, while in previous films he has usually impersonated playful, evil characters. Similarly for Cage: one associates him with characters of goodwill, but who are somehow depressed, while in *Face/Off* he plays the role of an openly evil man. It thus seems that only when Travolta and Cage exchange their faces can they start resembling their usual film personalities. The questions of who the subject is by himself and what his mask is thus get even more complicated. There is a gap between a subject and his face. The subject always has the wrong face; and *Face/Off* suggests that the subject might need the face of another to express his inner self.

In *Gattaca*, the problem of subjectivity in a future genetically controlled society also takes on another meaning when we consider one more pair – Vincent and his brother Anton, who is a genetically constructed Valid. While Jerome is a disabled Valid and thus limited in how he can use his genetic perfection, Anton is a supreme human being. The relationship between the two brothers is a very troubled one. From early childhood, they especially liked to compete in swimming; and once, when Vincent wins a competition and saves Anton from drowning, Anton becomes extremely resentful toward Vincent. If Jerome is portrayed as a somewhat depressed, but generally good Valid, Anton is presented as an evil one. But the crucial question here is: why is Anton, who is in all ways a perfect man, envious and resentful toward an In-Valid like Vincent? The obvious answer psychoanalysis would give is that envy is a sign that the subject is split – barred, branded by a lack. This also gives us a more optimistic view of a future genetically controlled society. The subject will be able to deal with the deadlocks of this society precisely because he or she is a split subject. The lack that marks the subject is not an obstacle, but the very condition of the subject's creativity.

This lack is ultimately generated by the antagonistic tension between meaning and *jouissance*. When Lacan says that subjects are "enjoying speech qua *jouissance* of speech",[8] he claims that the subject obtains a certain *jouissance* (even happiness) through speech. The subject, however, approaches this meaningless *jouissance* through the fantasy screen: the aim of a fantasy scenario is precisely to mask and to filter the traumatic impact of this *jouissance*. Here, we can again take the example of hate speech. The subject who utters violent words forms a fantasy scenario of hatred toward a particular Other in order to cover up the fact that he or she is unable to confer any meaning on the traumatic experience of the Other's *jouissance*. And, far from reinscribing these particular traumatic encounters with the Other's *jouissance* into the field of meaning, the analytic interpretation has to reassert the gap that forever separates *jouissance* from this field of meaning, i.e. to reintroduce a certain "this says nothing" in regard to the subject's *jouissance*.[9]

The point of Lacan's well-known statement that there is no sexual relationship is precisely that the subject's relationship to the Other is always inadequate, even perverse, insofar as the subject relates to the Other as object *a*, the embodiment of some excessive *jouissance*. In regard to the sexual relationship, Lacan makes further puzzling statements by saying that it "doesn't stop not being written", which means that nothing can be said of the sexual relationship in speech. The subject's love relationship primarily concerns "the encounter in the partner of symptoms and affects, of everything that marks in each of us the trace of his exile – not as subject but as speaking – his exile from the sexual relationship".[10] In other words, the sexual relationship fails, because we encounter in another subject the object *a*, the object of desire and drive, around which he or she forms his or her symptoms and through which he or she also enjoys. However, the symptoms and affects encountered in the subject create the *illusion* that the "sexual relationship stops not being written", i.e. that the encounter is inscribed in our destiny. This is a moment of contingency: at the stroke of great love everything is suspended and we have the mirage of a sexual relationship. At that moment the impossibility of the sexual relationship, articulated as "doesn't stop being written", appears as a necessity, as something that "doesn't stop being written"; i.e. we think that the encounter had to happen and that the relationship is to last.

Love is a contingent encounter of two subjects, or, better, of their "unconscious knowledges"[11] that target in each other what they do not have. At the moment of this mirage-like encounter, we do not want to know that the encounter is contingent and that our desire for the other will only be sustained if we continue missing each other. In this search for what is in our partner more than him- or herself (his or her being), love easily gives way to hate. And when we hate someone, we also do not want to know about the contingent nature of our encounter. We desperately try to identify some substantive trait we dislike in the others (their culture, their skin color, the smell of their food, etc.) so that we can take our hatred of them as grounded in an objective necessity.

Is there a way to resolve the puzzles of love and hate? At the end of the seminar *Encore*, Lacan says, "to know what your partner will do is not a proof of love". Thus, love can flourish only because we are split subjects, i.e. only because we know nothing about each other's being, which also means that there is no love without the impossibility attached to it. In love, too, we must accept that, in the end, it "says nothing"; that is why for centuries people created their best artwork in trying to give meaning to it, i.e. to fill its lack.

So let us conclude this book with another reference to Klein – this time not to Calvin himself, but to his daughter Marsha who, in a *Vanity Fair* interview, was asked if being the daughter of such a famous man does not cause difficulties in her love life.[12] In her answer, she jokingly located the problem in the fact that the last thing she usually sees before pulling down the pants of her lover is her father's name (the designer's mark on the underwear), thereby recalling Lacan's thesis from the last page of his *Seminar XI* that "any shelter in which may be established a viable, temperate relation of one sex to the other necessitates the intervention . . . of that medium known as the paternal metaphor".[13] Is then Lacan's ultimate lesson that this intervention of the paternal metaphor is irrevocable? Our wager is the exact opposite of this resigned acceptance of the paternal authority: the fact that *jouissance* ultimately "says nothing", that the gap that separates it from the domain of meaning (sustained and guaranteed by the phallic signifier) is irreducible, leads us to imagine the sexually aroused Marsha Klein tearing down her lover's pants without being compelled to confront her father's name as the last thing she saw before being engulfed by the abyss of *jouissance*.

NOTES

1. Ulrich Beck, "Politics of Risk Society", in *The Politics of Risk Society*, ed. Jane Franklin, Cambridge: Polity Press 1998, p. 14.
2. Recently, the American male movement called "The Promise Keepers" decided to prevent the further decline of the patriarchal family by encouraging men to take charge of their families again. It holds that men first need to apologize to their wives for placing the burden of leading the family on their shoulders and then should retake control. The ideology of this movement is that, by nature, men should have the power in their families, so that, when regaining control of them, they are only assuming a position that was always supposed to be theirs. Another presupposition of this movement is that families should stick together and allow the father to reign, however bad family relations might be. One can imagine that a woman whose alcoholic, irresponsible husband suddenly wants to "keep his promise" would not be thus relieved from the family burdens, but merely assigned another one—to tidy her man's throne.
3. When, in various public surveys, young people are asked about their views on family life, they often point out that when they grow up they want to create a much more traditional family than the one in which they have been brought up: their parents were rarely at home, they were exhausted by work, they had little time for their children, and their marriages usually broke up. Since today's youth have already experienced the "freedom" that comes with the non-traditional family life style, it is hard to imagine that they would be willing to accept the forms of submission and gender inequality that existed in the traditional patriarchal family. Young people have a paradoxical desire to live in a firm but tolerant community. Here, corporations like Microsoft offer themselves as an alternative both to the permissive and to the traditional families. Such corporations present themselves as a permissive version of the traditional family: they offer new types of "friendly" authorities, who encourage people to play with their creativity and who do not discipline their eccen-

tricity; but once people's work is perceived to be unprofitable, the punishment can be most "unfriendly".

4. See Douglas Coupland, *Microserfs*, London: Flamingo 1996.
5. Microsoft has dominated the computer software industry in recent years, and many fear that its power will significantly expand in the future to control other telecommunication systems worldwide. Some compare the power that Microsoft might have in the twenty-first century with the power the British Empire had in the nineteenth century and the Russian Communist Party in the twentieth. In his campaign for consumer rights, Ralph Nader has been organizing a series of conferences on Microsoft, which analyze the strategies Microsoft uses to prevent other computer companies from competing with it. Paradoxically, representatives of competitive companies were very reluctant to publicly express their disagreements with Microsoft, since they knew very well that Bill Gates can ruin them at any time. Gates's power is that he has huge amounts of money and can easily buy from competing firms; but his strength also comes from the fact that he is very flexible: "He will not draw his sword if he can offer his carrot." See *Independent*, 18 November 1997.
6. For a detailed analysis of the shift from the father-like authority to the brother's, see Juliet Flower MacCannell, *The Regime of the Brother: After Patriarchy*, London: Routledge 1991.
7. The French film *Les Yeux sans visage* (Georges Franju, 1959) also deals with the problem of changing one's face. Here we have a doctor who experiments with transplanting faces. When his daughter damages her face in a car accident, the doctor kills a young girl, steals her face and transplants it on to the daughter's. But the transplanted skin quickly deteriorates, so the doctor kills another girl. And when this new face starts falling apart, the doctor again finds another young victim. Finally, the daughter realizes what her father is doing; she saves the last victim and reveals her father's crimes. By doing so, the daughter "saves her face", i.e. her honesty.
8. Jacques Lacan, *On Feminine Sexuality: The Limits of Love and Knowledge (Book XX – Encore 1972–1973)*, trans. Bruce Fink, New York: Norton 1998, pp. 126–7.
9. See Jacques-Alain Miller, "Le monologue de *l'apparole*", *La Cause Freudienne* 34 (1996).
10. Lacan, *On Feminine Sexuality*, p. 145.
11. Ibid., p. 144.
12. I thank Sina Najafi for telling me this anecdote.
13. Jacques Lacan, *The Four Fundamental Concepts of Psycho-Analysis*, trans. Alan Sheridan, New York: Norton 1977, p. 276.

INDEX